The Reduced Shakespeare Company's

The Complete Works of

William Shakespeare

(abridged)

by Jess Borgeson, Adam Long, and Daniel Singer

edited by Professor J. M. Winfield

APPLAUSE BOOKS

The Complete Works of William Shakespeare (abridged)

Edited by Professor J.M. Winfield

Library of Congress Catalog-in-Publication Data

Borgeson, Jess
    The Reduced Shakespeare Company's The Complete Works of William Shakespeare (abridged) / by Jess Borgeson, Adam Long and Daniel Singer; edited by J.M. Winfield.
        p. cm.
    Incorporates all 37 of Shakespeare's plays into a 2 hour play
    ISBN 1-55783-157-2: $7.95
        1. Shakespeare, William, 1564-1616--Adaptations. I. Long, Adam.
II. Singer, Daniel. III. Winfield, J.M. IV. Title.
PR2879.B67 1994
822.3'3--dc20   93-38692
                                           CIP

British Library Catalog in Publication Data

A catalogue record for this book is available from the British Library

APPLAUSE BOOKS
211 WEST 71ST STREET   406 VALE ROAD
NEW YORK, NY 10023   TONBRIDGE KENT TN9 1XR
PHONE 212-496-7511   PHONE 0732 357755
FAX 212-721-2856   FAX: 0732 770219

FIRST APPLAUSE PRINTING: 1994

"WHY? A MAN THAT MAKES HIM SHALL REALL,
HIMSELF, HOW MANY TOWNS HIS LIKENESS ——?"

THE ALTO RELIEVO

iii

*This book is dedicated to all the brave men and women
who have lost their lives
in the performance of Shakespeare's works.*

Table of Contents

Frontispiece: We see here why Shakespeare decided to become an immortal playwright: babes, babes, babes! And is it just my, your esteemed editor's, imagination, or is Shakespeare's Head MUCH too small for his body?

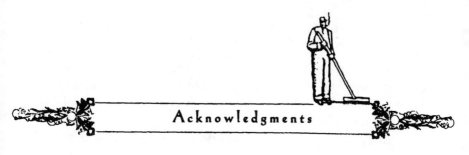

Acknowledgments

Throughout the 12 years of the Reduced Shakespeare Company's existence, many people have made contributions, large and small, to the script of *The Complete Works* and to the development of the RSC. They have never received a dime from us "authors" for their input, and they're not going to now, but we thought we'd take a few lines to thank them anyway. We'd like first to thank all the former members of the RSC whose names we can still remember from those blurry bygone days: the other founding members of the Company, Michael Fleming and Barbara Reinertson, for their work in creating the original half-hour *Hamlet;* Erroll Ross and Jim and Marilyn Letchworth; and David Springhorn, who played a large role in refining *Hamlet*, particularly in discovering that OOB is BOO spelt backwards *and* upside down. We'd like to thank Chris Springhorn for going into labor at a crucial point in the Company's history. Thanks also to Jack Tate for coming up with a once-in-a-lifetime idea; to Dan McLaughlin and Mark Sellin for *Julius Caesar*; to the Doug Anthony All-Stars for teaching us how to hit an audience member; to Tom Stoppard for bringing Bardian abridgment into the modern idiom; to Phyllis Patterson and the Living History Centre for their constant support and extended costume loans; and to costumer Sa Winfield for being much funnier than we are.

We have always encouraged our technical crew and support staff to make creative contributions to the show, so we are probably indebted to Scott Ewing, Scott Barringer, Ted Simmons, Marla Wilson, Heidi Metcalf, Kent Elofson, Jack Foster, Steve Schon, Sooz Glenn, Hughes Hall, McMike O'Hara, Shawn Wellyn, Karl Hamann, Vernon Marshal and even Graham Wright for their ideas as well as their tireless work on the show. Thanks also to our generous Scottish hosts during our first trip to the Edinburgh Festival Fringe—Christine, Rebecca, Peter, Davey, and Leslie—for helping us to fine-tune *Macbeth*.

In preparing the book, despite the editor's claims to the contrary, we are indebted to two other works: Gary Taylor's *Reinventing Shakespeare* and Henry Beard's *Latin for All Occasions*.

And finally, as always, very special thanks to Greg Moore.

Introduction

It is part of a long and hallowed tradition when publishing Shakespeare's works to have a famous Shakespearean actor, director, or other literary giant of the day compose an introduction to the collection. In an effort to keep that tradition alive, the Reduced Shakespeare Company sent an enquiry to the most acclaimed young Shakespearean actor/director of our day, Mr. Kenneth Branagh:

Dear Kenneth Branagh;

We are three Californians who are writing the Complete Works of William shakespeare. We thought It would be really cool if you would write the Introduction.

Please keep it to 500 words or less

Love,
Adam Jess Daniel
Reduced Shakespeare Co

Surprisingly, Mr. Branagh did not reply. The RSC then briefly considered asking Sir Ian McKellan, Sir Laurence Olivier, or Sir John Gielgud to contribute the Introduction, but couldn't remember which of the three was alive, which was dead, and which was nearly dead, and so decided to give it a miss. Taking another tack, the RSC thought that, since Shakespeare is forever bound in history's remembrance with the reign of Queen Elizabeth I, perhaps her modern namesake, Queen Elizabeth II, would care to introduce this contemporary edition of "Elizabethan" drama:

Dear Queen Elizabeth:

We are three Californians who are writing the Complete Works of William Shakespeare. We thought it would be really cool if you would write the introduction.

Please keep it to 500 words or less.

Love,
Adam Jess David
Reduced Shakespeare Co.

The RSC was greatly disappointed to find that the British Royal Family has become so paranoid that they no longer answer even the increasingly rare NICE letters like this one. Professor J. M. Winfield, the esteemed editor of this book, thought that perhaps an American artist would be more receptive to the task of writing the Introduction. He wrote the following request to one such artist, and received polite regrets:

Professor J. M. Winfield

August 24, 1993

Heather Locklear
Famous Person

Dear Ms. Locklear:

I am currently editing a new publication of *The Complete Works of William Shakespeare.* It is a work of tremendous scholarship and massive ambition, to which some of the greatest literary minds of our generation, myself included, have contributed.

We are at present screening hundreds of writers, poets, actors, and directors, one of whom will be offered the honor of composing an Introduction to the Book. As a featured actress in such ground-breaking works as *Swamp Thing, Dynasty, T. J. Hooker* (where you worked with one of the great Shakespearean actors of our time, Sir William Shatner), and now *Melrose Place,* we feel you could bring a truly unique perspective to the ageless works of the Bard of Stratford-Upon-Avon.

You are also just about the only famous person I know personally. Remember, we were in the same Spanish class in high school, and we rode the same bus to junior high? I was the precocious, slightly effeminate drama geek, and you were the incredibly popular future-celebrity Homecoming Queen-type whose mere presence in the same room made me quake in my Wallabees and my tongue cleave to the roof of my mouth?

We sincerely hope that, for the sake of Shakespearean scholarship, you will consider contributing an Introduction to our Book. Perhaps we could discuss the project over dinner at my place. I have some delightful Shakespearean etchings which might be of interest to you.

Sincerely,

Professor J. M. Winfield

September 7, 1993

Professor J. M. Winfield
c/o Applause Books
221 W. 71st St.
New York, NY 10023

Dear Professor:

Thank you for very flattering request, that I pen an
introduction to your edition of *The Complete Works of William
Shakespeare*. Unfortunately, I am unable to grant your
request at this time, due to an unusually busy schedule. In
addition to shooting the current season of *Melrose Place*, I
am overseeing publication of a German translation of the
complete dramatic *oeuvre* of Anton Chekov while simultaneously
acting as a consultant to a new edition of the Oxford English
Dictionary.

I do, in fact, remember you from high school. "Slightly
effeminate" is an understatement, and "geek" does not begin
to describe my recollection of you. By the way, has the skin
problem cleared up yet?

Please attempt no further contact with me, as I have obtained
a temporary restraining order barring you from approaching
within 100 yards of my person.

Yours

Heather Locklear

Heather Locklear, Famous American

The conclusion to be drawn here is that the timeless works of William Shakespeare need no introduction. Their genius speaks for itselves.

Or will, after a few grammatically impeccable prefatory notes by the Authors, the Publisher, and the esteemed Editor of this Book.

PREFACE

Editor's Note

It is with hearty concupiscence and much balneal flatulence that I welcome you, humble reader, to this tome. In the quaternian centuries twixt the maternal parturition of the Bard of Stratford-upon-Avon and these latter days of cultural *gavage*, many an editor has entrumpassed the gargantuan task of entombing these greatest of all manifestations of the Melopmenean muse: *The Complete Works of William Shakespeare*. It is a burden I have shouldered with superciliousness and fustian sesquipedality. In short, I have tried to keep it simple.

In preparing the Shakespearean text for this book, I have found the Cambridge, Riverside and Oxford *Complete Works* texts, the highly-respected Temple Notes (as revised by Prof. Oeufpate), Mr. Kermode's *Four Centuries of Shakespearian Criticism,* and especially Caroline Spurgeon's seminal article, "Shakespeare's Iterative Imagery," to be completely useless. In fact, I have used no books, articles, reference or research materials of any kind in preparing the text. To be perfectly honest, I haven't even read a book for several years now, but I have an over-achieving thesaurus program on my Macintosh that spews out a half-dozen five-syllable synonyms for "fart" at the click of a button, so why even bother improving my intellect? I spend most of my time watching public access programming and "Beavis and Butthead" on late-night television, wishing that they were showing more live female mud wrestling instead. Sure, I was an English Lit major once, but my life since then has been an intellectual cul-de-sac. I got so burned out reading all 465 zillion cantos of Edmund Spenser's goddamn "Faerie Queene" in three coffee-bloated sleepless nights in college that just the mention of "English Literature" these days quite literally makes me want to throw up.

But I digress.

Since the initial compilation of Shakespeare's plays appeared as the First Folio of 1623, there have been some 652 published editions of the Bard's *Complete Works*.[1] "What possible justification can there be," you ask, "for this new volume?"

To which I reply: "It's much, much shorter."

While Shakespeare is unquestionably the greatest playwright ever to doctor a dactyl, any ninth-grader will tell you that he simply used too many words. As Polonius so punctiliously posits, "Brevity is the soul of wit." (Hamlet II. ii. 97 or so). This edition is the first to wholeheartedly acknowledge and embrace that axiomatic fact. Whereas the Oxford *Complete Works* runs to some 1,258,762 words,[2] this slim opuscule contains only 32,044 words[3] and a couple of pretty pictures. We have expunged much of Shakespeare's subtle psychological insight, his carefully spun subplots, his well-honed social satire, and skipped right to the sex and killing. What joy to rediscover the ample amphigory of Mercutio's meretriciousness, the obstreperous callithump of Hotspur's hectoring, or the importunate innocence of Imogen's ingenuousness without encountering the execrable effluvium of editorial excess!

To this approach, if I may speak prosopopeially, Shakespeare himself would say, "Excellent swell!"

We hope this work succeeds in its Atlantean endeavor: to transcend the bibliomaniac bombast of the pedagogue and reveal the simple beauty of the Bard. May reading this book always bring you wisdom, insight, and pudendal tumescence of the highest order.

Professor J. M. Winfield

---

[1] A wild guess.

[2] Also a wild guess.

[3] An extremely accurate figure, I counted them myself.

Publisher's Preface to the Foreword to the Authors' Notes

It was a simple idea at the beginning: "Authors' Notes." Jess Borgeson, Adam Long and Daniel Singer, the authors of the script of *The Complete Works of William Shakespeare (abridged),* would each write a brief note providing their perspective on the text.

The whole thing has gone terribly, terribly wrong. You may wish to avoid the train wreck altogether and skip directly to the script, which begins on page 1.

For those of you who plow bravely on through the next few pages, be forewarned that Shakespeare surely spoke of Professor Winfield, the esteemed editor of this book, when he wrote, "Thus he his special nothing ever prologues." (*All's Well That End's Well,* II.1.91)

Foreword to the Authors' Notes

In a moment, you will be reading the "Authors' Notes" to *The Complete Works of William Shakespeare (abridged).* As your editor, I just wanted to take this opportunity to wish you well in your reading of them. The co-authors are fascinating people, and their comments are certain to be illuminating. Jess, for example, will probably feel sorry for himself a lot, make a political joke or two, and then quote something in Latin. Adam, his finger always on the pulse of modern culture, will place the script in a socio-philosophical context that only he can understand. Daniel, in his down-to-earth way, will no doubt bore us all to tears by actually discussing issues related to the script of *The Complete Works.* Let us turn the page, and see how this captivating commentary plays out, after which you, humble reader, will be treated to more lofty and enlightened analysis by me, your somewhat less humble editor...

Authors' Notes

Jess Borgeson

Co-writing *The Complete Works of William Shakespeare (abridged)* is unquestionably the crowning achievement of my life. Which is really depressing, as I'm only 32 years old. The prospect that I may never match this ridiculous piece of fluff we knocked off in a few days seven years ago horrifies me. Will the rest of my life be a vain attempt to recapture past glories, telling my grandchildren exaggerated tales about the good old days with the RSC through decaying teeth, my breath stinking of cheap whiskey bought with my meager Social Security check? Or is there really hope in this cruel world for a former Shakespearean sex symbol with thinning hair and a meaningless undergraduate degree whose résumé says things like, "Played the role of the Balcony in *Romeo and Juliet*?" I know the prospects look grim, but I'm sure I'll be fine. Just look at Ronald Reagan. When he couldn't cut it as an actor anymore, he quit and became *President.*

One word about my collaboration with Adam and Daniel on the script of *The Complete Works*. The creative interaction between the three of us was intense, fast-paced, absolutely electric. It is extremely difficult to sort out, seven years later, who wrote what, whose idea this or that bit was, but I know one thing for sure: the really funny stuff was all MINE.

So sweep on, you fat and greasy citizens! Revel in the splendor of our bounteous wit, keep us in mind for odd jobs around the house, and as the great Roman poet Virgil so aptly put it, *"Die dulce fruere."* *

---

* "Have a nice day."

Adam Long

I saw the best minds of my generation

destroyed by madness

Starving, hysterical, naked;

Dragging themselves through the negro

streets at dawn

Looking for an angry fix...

From "HOWL" by Allen Ginsberg

When I first read "HOWL," Ginsberg's words were like a slap in the head with a neon shovel. At the time, I was a kid living in Los Angeles and my comrades and I, inspired by the Marx Brothers and MTV, had just started condensing the complete works of William Shakespeare into the concise, pithy and eminently readable manuscript you hold before you now. At first, the task of such a massive condensation seemed hopeless, and I approached the words of the Bard meekly, cautiously, even with a sense of reverence. But the night I read "HOWL" I was electrified by reckless despair. I knew we weren't the best minds of our generation, but we were starving and hysterical. And we often went without clothes. The next day we assaulted the Bard of Avon like cultural guerillas on steroids. We tore madly into volume after volume of the Bard's work. Blindly. Insanely. Embarrassingly. Now the smoke has cleared. The deed is done.

May the Bard forgive us.

Daniel Singer

In 1981 I took a copy of Shakespeare's *Hamlet*, tore out a few select pages, attacked them with a grease pencil, hired three total strangers and produced a sixteenth-century vaudeville show. The connection between that event and the publishing of this book is bizarre and intangible. If the crowds had booed and thrown vegetables, as we had anticipated, this "play" (I use the term loosely) would never have been created. But audiences of the last quarter of the twentieth century apparently possessed an urgent need to see Shakespeare performed as if it were a Tex Avery cartoon, so the Reduced Shakespeare Company thrived. Fortunately we were young and indestructable, and seven years of doing aerobic choreography in direct sunlight on outdoor stages, eating dust, sweating through three layers of costumes, being interrupted by parades, croaking through laryngitis, colds, and nodes, and dragging our tired butts all over the world, has given birth to this script. Go figure.

Most of what we did on stage is here in print, but much of the physical shtick, when described, becomes meaningless. We couldn't ask readers to find the point of a comment like "Hamlet and Claudius leap at each other and bounce off each other's torso," so our editor has judiciously weeded out "business that is not integral to the continuity." On the other hand, the stage direction, "Juliet begins to convulse, vomits on several people in the front row, and finally flips over unconscious," is vital to our our story, and it is fun to imagine a live actor actually doing this.

Reading the *Complete Works*, is, then, a very different experience from seeing it performed live. Slapstick tends to steamroll over subtler forms of humor, so we are glad to see that some jokes we wrote ten years ago might finally be appreciated. Also, there is excellent shock value in seeing a Great Shakespearean Scene reduced to two lines. I have noticed, however, that some of the verbal word-play of "Titus Androgynous" doesn't work if read silently, so this is probably a great script to read aloud with a group of drunken friends.

Fortunately for us, the material has been performed hundreds of times in front of audiences around the world, so most of the bugs have been worked out. Some bugs took up permanent residence in *Troilus and Cressida*, however, and there's no getting rid of them.

Lastly, there is a wealth of material written for the show that has never been performed. Countless treatments of the Comedies; a "serious" treatment of *King Lear*; *Timon of Athens* starring a member of the audience who is required to remove his clothing; and a version of *Hamlet* where the main character is obsessed with socks and meat. Don't ask. You don't want to read that stuff.

William Shakespeare

When the boys first approached me about writing an "Author's Note" for this book I was overwhelmed and honored. The condensations within these pages are puerile, shallow, and absurd, and that's exactly why this volume is so important and meaningful. Let's face it, when you're a playwright who's been dead for a few hundred years it's difficult to compete culturally in this age of MTV and Nintendo. Iambic pentameter isn't "hip" these days. Three quatrains and a rhyming couplet are no match for digitally sampled erotic heaving and black and white super-8 of fishnet stockings and pierced nipples. Looking back on it now I would have done things differently...O, so differently. *Mais c'est la vie.*

There are a few people I'd like to thank. I'd like to thank Chris Marlowe and Ben Johnson for all the support and input they gave me over the years. I'd like to thank the Dark Lady (just to be cryptic). But mostly, I'd like to thank Adam, Daniel, and Jess, without whom my work would surely have vanished from the cultural map along with Hula-Hoops and the Water Wiggle. Adam, Daniel, and Jess...I love you. Had I a womb and fallopian tubes, yea verily would I carry your collective baby.

Finally, to you the reader: I hope, as you peruse these pages, you will judge that I have acquitted myself honorably. I have only endeavored, through the veil of time, to entertain and amuse and to be as you demanded I should:

> What you have charged me with, that have I done,
> And more, much more; the time will bring it out.
> 'Tis past; and so am I.
> The wheel is come full circle; I am here.
> Put your hands all over my body.
> Mmmmmm...   *King Lear* (V.iii.160-174)

But enough of this. You have some serious reading ahead of you. And I have some serious decomposing to get back to. I pray you, enjoy.

Afterword to the Authors' Notes

Wasn't that enthralling? Before we move on, I'd like to say a few words about the Authors' Notes you've just read. If we read between the lines, each note provides incisive insight into the co-author's character. Jess' note, for example, is prettily written but lacking in substance. His hogging of credit for the show is indicative of a massive inferiority complex, while his attempt at political humor is both out-of-place and badly dated. His use of Latin is, however, undeniably impressive. Conversely, Adam's note is passionate and powerful, but so obscure as to be rendered practically meaningless. His citation of Ginsberg seems woefully *passé*, and the nihilistic philosophy at odds with his essential nature. Daniel's note is enlightening, utilitarian, compellingly simple and therefore completely unreadable.

I will not stoop to discussing the surprise appearance of the note from "William Shakespeare," as it was quite obviously ghostwritten.

Reader's Note

I'm just an average guy. I bought this book in the checkout line at Safeway, along with two bags of Nacho Cheese Doritos and a six-pack of Bud, and I'm reading it during the commercials of Monday Night Football.

So far, I think it's crap.

You'd better get onto the good stuff, the "To be or not to be," the "Wherefore art thou Romeo," and all that, or I'm going to find the people responsible for this miserable publication and beat the living bejeezus out of them.

You got it, eggheads? Now MOVE IT!

You, Humble Reader

By Jess Borgeson, Adam Long, and Daniel Singer

with additional material by Reed Martin

All inquiries concerning performance rights should be addressed to: Writers and Artists Agency, 19 West 44th Street, Suite 1000, New York, NY 10036, Attn: William Craver

The Reduced Shakespeare Company production of *The Complete Works of William Shakespeare (abridged)* was first performed (more or less in its entirety) by the authors on June 19, 1987, at the Paramount Ranch in Agoura, California, and subsequently at the 1987 Edinburgh Festival Fringe in Scotland. The original cast:

Jess Borgeson ....Jess Borgeson

Adam Long ....Adam Long

Daniel Singer..Daniel Singer

NOTE: The script is written for three actors. Where Shakespearean characters appear in the script, the character name is preceded by the actor's initial: e.g. A/JULIET means Adam is playing Juliet, D/ROMEO means Daniel is playing Romeo, J/HAMLET means Jess is playing Hamlet, etc. More or less "Shakespearean" dialogue appears in quotation marks (" ").

The Complete Works of

William Shakespeare

(abridged)

Act 1

(The preshow music, the 'Jupiter' section of Gustav Holz' 'The Planets,' reaches its crashing climax. Lights come up on the stage. The set consists of a backdrop representing an Elizabethan theater in the fashion of Shakespeare's Globe, with entrances upstage right and left. Stage right there is a 'Masterpiece Theater'-style narrator's chair, on which there sits a book: The Complete Works of William Shakespeare. *After a beat,* DANIEL, *ostensibly a house manager enters from the wings stage left.)*

DANIEL: Good evening, ladies and gentlemen, and welcome to the _____ Theater and tonight's performance by the Reduced Shakespeare Company. I have a few brief announcements before we get under way. The use of flash photography and the recording of this show by any means, audio or video, is strictly prohibited by the management. Also, please refrain from eating, drinking, or smoking—anything—during the performance. For your convenience, toilets are located in the lobby. Also, please take a moment now to locate the exit nearest your seat. *(Points to exits, in the manner of an airline flight attendant.)* Should the theater experience a sudden loss of pressure, oxygen masks *(Pulls one from his jacket pocket.)* will drop automatically. Simply place the mask over your nose and mouth, and continue to breathe normally. If you are at the theater with a small child,[1] please place your own mask on first, and let the little bugger fend for himself. At this time, I would like to introduce myself.

---

[1] *'with a small child'*; the RSC wishes to warn the readers that due to strong language, subversive concepts, and shabby scholarship, *The Complete Works of William Shakespeare (abridged)* may be unsuitable for very young children. Children must in fact be taller than this line:

...to enjoy the show.

The Compleat Wks of Willm Shkspr (Abridged)

My name is Daniel Singer of the Reduced Shakespeare Company, and tonight we are going to attempt a feat which we believe to be unprecedented in the history of theater. That is, to capture, in a single theatrical experience, the magic, the genius, the towering grandeur of 'The Complete Works of William Shakespeare.' Now we have a lot to get through tonight, so at this time I'd like to introduce a member of the Company who is one of California's preëminent Shakespearean scholars.[2] He has a bachelor's degree from the University of California at Berkeley, where I believe he read two books[3] about William Shakespeare. He is here tonight to provide a brief preface to 'The Complete Works of William Shakespeare (abridged).' Please welcome me in joining Mr. Jess Borgeson.

(JESS enters in a tweedy suit and spectacles. He picks up the book from the armchair and shakes hands with DANIEL, who sits in the armchair to listen.)

JESS: Thank you, Daniel, and good evening, ladies and gentlemen. *(Clinging to the 'Complete Works' book, he begins professorially, as if lecturing a class of students.)* William Shakespeare: playwright, poet, actor, philosopher; a man whose creative and literary genius have had an immeasurably profound influence upon the consciousness and culture of the entire English-speaking world.[4] And yet, how much do we inhabitants

---

[2] *'preëminent Shakespearean scholars'*; he's so preëminent, in fact, that he insisted on the fancy umlaut over the second 'e' in 'preëminent.'

[3] *'two books'*; research into Jess' library records at Berkeley indicate the two books to be *Shakespeare for Tots With Hoppy the Frog* and Norman Rabkin's *Reinterpretations of Elizabethan Drama,* which Jess apparently used as a kitchen table in his student apartment.

[4] *'the entire English-speaking world'*; Shakespeare is of course well-known in the non-English speaking world as well; witness the success of such foreign-language films as Akira Kurosawa's *Ran* (based on *King Lear* and spoken in Japanese), Grigori Kosintsev's *Hamlet* (based on *Hamlet* and spoken in Russian), and Long Dong Silver's *King Henry the Eighteen Inches* (based on the Shakespeare-Fletcher collaboration and incorporating sections of Shakespeare's narrative poem, 'A Lover's Complaint.' We forget what language they spoke in that one.)

of the twentieth century really know and appreciate the tremendous body of work contained in this single volume? Too little, I would argue. I believe I could illustrate this point by conducting a brief poll here, among our audience. *(to the light booth)* If I may have the house lights for just a moment, please?

(The house lights come up.)

Now, you are a theater-going crowd, no doubt of above-average cultural and literary awareness, and yet if I may just have a brief show of hands, how many of you here tonight have ever seen or read any play by William Shakespeare? Any contact at all with the Bard, just raise your hands... *(Almost everyone raises a hand. JESS shrinks away to confer, sotto voce, with DANIEL.)* I think they might know more than we do, maybe we better get outta here.

DANIEL: Don't worry about it.

JESS: No, we should really start running NOW.

DANIEL: They don't know Shakespeare from shinola, just keep going.

JESS: What should I do?

DANIEL *(mouthing)*: Narrow it down.

JESS: What?

DANIEL *(whispering)*: Narrow it down.

JESS *(to audience)*: Let's see if we can narrow it down a bit, shall we? How many of you have ever seen or read, let's say, 'All's Well That Ends Well?' *(Perhaps a third of the audience raises* *their hands.)* Yes, that seems to be separating the wheat from the chaff rather nicely. Let's see if we can find out who the true Shakespeare trivia champs are tonight. Has anybody ever seen or read 'King John?' 'King John,' anyone?

(ADAM, in street garb, raises his hand in the third row. JESS spots him.)

JESS: You have, really? Would you mind telling us what it's about?

ADAM: It's about a hunchback.[5]

JESS *(momentarily silent, then pointing an accusing finger at* ADAM*)*: This is exactly what I'm talking about. Oh, right, you laugh, ladies and gentlemen, you scoff, but let he among you who is free from sin live in a glass house! For that face, ladies and gentlemen, that face represents all your faces. *(JESS leaves the stage and begins to bear down on* ADAM.*)* That empty brain represents your empty brains. Those glazed eyes are your glazed eyes, these teeth *(grabbing* ADAM'S *face)* are your teeth, and they cry out, 'FLOSS ME!' *(returning to stage)* Ladies and gentlemen, I submit to you that our society's collective capacity to comprehend—much less attain—the genius of a William Shakespeare has been systematically compromised by computers, vandalized by video games, saturated with soap operas and dealt its death blow by Dan Quayle.[6] But have no

---

[5] *'hunchback'*; Adam is confused...not for the last time. He has of course mixed up King John with Richard III, a character made famous in the twentieth century by Sir Charles Laughton's portrayal in *The Hunchback of Notre Dame,* and of course its sequel, *The Knute Rockne Story.*

[6] *'Dan Quayle'*; the text presented throughout this manuscript has been 'timeless-ized;' that is, most political, topical, and local references, which are ubiquitous in the script and would be constantly updated by the RSC, have been made general in order to keep the script from becoming dated (see, for example, footnote 1193). This joke is the one exception, as the authors couldn't think of anybody in the Clinton Administration as dumb as Dan Quayle.

fear! The Reduced Shakespeare Company is here! *(He is beginning to metamorphose into a fire-and-brimstone evangelist.)* We descend among you on a mission from God and the literary muse, to spread the holy word of the Bard to the masses. To help you take those first halting steps OUT of the twentieth century quagmire of Donahue, Geraldo and Oprah Jessy Raphael, and into the future! A glorious future! A future where this book *(indicating the 'Complete Works')* will be found in every hotel room in the world! This is my dream, ladies and gentlemen, and it begins here, tonight. Join us in taking those first steps down the path toward the brave new world of intellectual redemption by opening your hearts.

(DANIEL picks up a plate and begins to pass it among the audience, soliciting donations.)

Yes, please open your hearts—and your pocketbooks. Or simply charge your donations to your MasterCard or Visa by phoning 1-800-THE BARD right now! Give us your cash, if we be friends, and deduct it when the tax year ends! On with the show and may the Bard be with you! Thank you, and Hallelujah!!

(The house lights fade as DANIEL returns to the stage, shakes JESS' hand and exchanges the collection plate for the 'Complete Works' book. JESS finds a large bill in the plate and tucks it in his pocket as he exits.)

DANIEL: Those of you who own a copy of this book know that no collection is complete without a brief biography of the life of William Shakespeare. Providing this portion of the show will be the third member of the Reduced Shakespeare Company; please welcome to the stage Mr. Adam Long.

(ADAM *comes to the stage. As he shakes* DANIEL'S *hand, he drops a small stack of 3x5 index cards: his notes. He hastily picks them up.*)

DANIEL: Oops, sorry. Let me help you...

ADAM: No, don't touch them. They go in an order.

DANIEL: Okay, okay. *(Sits in chair.)*

ADAM *(trying to quickly put his notes back in order)*: I've just been taking a few notes on Shakespeare's life so we could get the show off to a good start, so you could know all the stuff he did an' everything...

DANIEL *(sotto voce)*: Just get on with it.

ADAM: Okay, okay. *(He begins reading from the index cards.)* William Shakespeare. William Shakespeare was born in 1564 in the town of Stratford-upon-Avon, Warwickshire. The third of eight children, he was the eldest son of John Shakespeare, a locally prominent merchant, and Mary Arden,[7] daughter of a Roman... *(flips to the next card)* ...Catholic member of the landed gentry. In 1582 he married Anne Hathaway,[8] a farmer's daughter...heh. He is supposed to have left Stratford after he was caught poaching in the deer park of a local justice of the peace. *(next card)* Shakespeare arrived in London in 1588. By 1592, he

---

[7] *'Mary Arden'*; recent research suggests that Mary Arden met her future husband while plying her trade in door-to-door cosmetic sales. All of Warwickshire recognized her cheery voice at the door: 'Ding-dong! Mary of Stratford-upon-Avon calling!'

[8] *'Anne Hathaway'*; a role later revived to great acclaim on American television's *The Beverly Hillbillies.*

had achieved success as an actor and a playwright. After 1608 his dramatic production lessened, and it seems that he spent more time in Stratford. *(next card)* There he dictated to his secretary, Rudolf Hess, the work 'Mein Kampf,' in which he set forth his program for the restoration of Germany to a dominant position in Europe. After reoccupying the Rhineland zone between France and Germany, and annexing Austria, the Sudetenland and the remainder of Czechoslovakia *(next card)*, Shakespeare invaded Poland on September 1, 1939, thus precipitating World War II. *(to DANIEL)* I never knew that before. *(DANIEL gestures to him to wrap it up. ADAM reads rapidly.)* Shakespeare remained in Berlin when the Russians entered the city, and committed suicide with his mistress, Eva Braun. *(next card)* He lies buried in the church at Stratford.[9] Thank you.

(ADAM bows. DANIEL rises, shakes his hand and hurries him offstage.)

DANIEL: Now, without further ado, the Reduced Shakespeare Company is proud to prevent 'The Complete Works of William Shakespeare (abridged).'

(Blackout. A pretentious heavy-metal version of 'Greensleeves' crashes through the sound system. The music ends with an enormous cymbal crash. A light comes up to reveal JESS in Shakespearean attire and Converse high-top canvas sneakers, sitting in the Masterpiece Theater chair and holding the

---

[9] *'buried in the church at Stratford'*; a word about Shakespeare's grave. Many a journalist has asked the authors whether Shakespeare is spinning in his grave over the alleged 'heresy' of the RSC's *Complete Works.* A pilgrimage to Stratford-Upon-Avon in 1990 afforded the authors the opportunity to check. No seismic activity was detected, although the RSC did learn that the clerics at Trinity Church get very upset when three badly-dressed Americans clamber onto the Bard's tomb and press their ears to the engraved slab.

"Shakespeare as a Boy of Twelve"
While Adam has confused Shakespeare with Adolf Hitler, this artist has
obviously confused him with Napoleon Bonaparte. Mistaking Shakespeare
for famous European military geniuses is a common error.

'Complete Works' book. He regards the audience smugly for a moment, opens the book, and reads.)

JESS: "All the world's a stage,
And all the men and women merely players.
They have their exits and their entrances
And one man in his time plays many parts."
One man in his time plays many parts. How true. Ladies and gentlemen, where better to begin our exploration of the complete works of the greatest of all English playwrights than in Verona, Italy—with two of his most beloved characters, Romeo and Juliet.

(ADAM and DANIEL enter, also in Elizabethan garb and sneakers, and begin warm-ups and stretches.)

Now, Adam and Daniel will be attempting to portray all of the major character roles in 'Romeo and Juliet,'[10] while I fill in with bits of narration. After extensive textual research and analysis, we of the Reduced Shakespeare Company have decided to begin our abbreviated version of 'Romeo and Juliet' with...the Prologue.

---

[10]*Romeo and Juliet* was first printed in 1597 under the following title: 'An excellent conceited Tragedie of Romeo and Juliet. As it hath been often (with great applause) plaid publiquely, by the right honourable the L. of Hunsdon his seruants.' Perhaps Shakespeare is allowed to be 'conceited,' being the greatest playwright ever, but that doesn't excuse wearing plaid in publique. It's a fashion felony.

The Compleat Wks of Willm Shkspr (Abridged)

ADAM AND DANIEL *(simultaneously, with synchronized gestures)*:
"Two households, both alike in dignity,
In fair Verona where we lay our scene,
From ancient grudge break to new mutiny
Where civil blood makes civil hands unclean.
From forth the fatal loins[11] of these two foes
A pair of star-cross'd lovers take their life;
Whose misadventured, piteous o'erthrows
Do, with their death, bury their parents' strife."

(They bow. DANIEL lifts ADAM into a balletic exit, then follows him off.)

JESS: Act One, Scene One: In the street meet two men tall and handsome,
One, Benvolio;[12] *(ADAM enters as BENVOLIO.)*
The other named Sampson. *(DANIEL enters as SAMPSON.)*
Their hatred fueled by an ancient feud
For one serves Capulet, the other Montague...d.

A/BEN *(singing)*: O, I like to rise when the sun she rises, early in the morning...

D/SAM *(singing simultaneously)*: O, I had a little doggie and his name was Mr. Jiggs, I sent him to the grocery store to fetch a pound of figs...

(They see each other. Simultaneously:)

---

[11] *'fatal loins'*; in Shakespeare's day, men's penises were often ground to a razor-sharp edge on a specially-designed lathe and used, not only as lethal weapons, but as everyday 'tools.' They would often be used as 'boning'-knives and, in seafaring circles, to clean fish—hence the term 'cod-piece'.

[12] *'Benvolio'*; a character now believed to have been modeled after the famous 14th century courtier/soldier/loan-shark Benny ("The Snake") Volio, who was in turn the bastard son of 13th century margarine magnate Sir Ben of Oleo.

A/BEN *(aside)*: Ooo, it's him. I hate his guts. I swear to God I'm gonna kill him.

D/SAM *(aside)*: Ooo, it's him. I hate his family, hate his dog, hate 'em all.

(They smile and bow to each other. As they cross to opposite sides of the stage, SAMPSON *bites his thumb at* BENVOLIO, *who trips* SAMPSON *in return.)*

A/BEN: "Do you bite your thumb at me, sir?

D/SAM: No sir, I do but bite my thumb.

A/BEN: Do you bite your thumb at me, sir?

D/SAM: No sir, I do not bite my thumb at you, sir, but I do bite my thumb. Do you quarrel, sir?

A/BEN: Quarrel, sir? No, sir.

D/SAM: But if you do, sir, I am for you. I serve as good a man as you.

A/BEN: No better.

D/SAM: Yes. Better.

A/BEN: You lie!

(They fly at each other. Massive fight scene. BENVOLIO *chases* SAMPSON *offstage.* BENVOLIO *flings a stunt-dummy* SAMPSON *onstage, stomps on it, twists its arm.* DANIEL *enters as the* PRINCE.*)*

D/PRINCE: Rebellious subjects, enemies to the peace.
    Profaners of this neighbor-stained steel.[13]
    You, Capulet, shall go along with me.
    Benvolio, come you this afternoon
    To know our farther[14] pleasure in this case.

    (D/PRINCE exits with dummy.)[15]

A/BEN: O where is Romeo? Saw you him today?
    Right glad I am he was not at this fray.
    But see, he comes!

    (DANIEL makes a grand entrance as ROMEO, wearing a very silly wig and wistfully sniffing at a rose.)

                    Romeo, he cried.
    I'll know his grievance or be much denied.
    Good morrow, coz.[16]

D/ROMEO: Is the day so young?

A/BEN: But new struck nine.

D/ROMEO: Ay, me. Sad hours seem long.

A/BEN: What sadness lengthens Romeo's hours?

---

[13] *'neighbor-stained steel'*; the image becomes disgustingly clear in light of the use of penises as weapons; see footnote 11 above.

[14] *'farther'*; originally 'farter's', excised for indecency by the Lord Mayor of London, c. 1599.

[15] *'dummy'*; the use of the dummy in Shakespeare is part of a long and hallowed Shakespearean tradition, first begun in the late Restoration and seen most recently in Mel Gibson's performance in the title role of Franco Zeffirelli's film version of *Hamlet*.

[16] *'coz'*; pinhead.

D/ROMEO: Not having that which, having, makes them short.

A/BEN: In love?[17]

D/ROMEO: Out.

A/BEN: Out of love?

D/ROMEO: Out of her favor where I am in love.

A/BEN: Alas that love, so gentle in his view,
Should be so rough and tyrannous[18] in proof.

D/ROMEO: Alas that love, whose view is muffl'd still,
Should without eyes see pathways to his will.

BOTH: O!

A/BEN: Go ye to the feast of Capulets.
There sups the fair Rosaline whom thou so lovest
With all the admired beauties of Verona.
Go thither[19] and compare her face with some that I shall show.
And I shall make thee think thy swan a crow. *(Exits.)*

D/ROMEO: I'll go along, no such sight to be shown,
But to rejoice in splendor of my own." *(Exits.)*

---

[17] *'In love?'*; in the 1598 Quarto, 'say *what?'*

[18] *'tyrannous'*; dinosaur-like.

[19] *'Go thither'*; why Benvolio, who is obviously one of Romeo's closest friends, suddenly starts calling him 'thither' is unclear. Samuel Johnson suggests that 'thither' should read 'zither,' and that Benvolio is suggesting Romeo ease his sorrows by practicing his music. A very dumb emendation. Rowe posited that Benvolio is trying to say 'sister,' but has a terrible lisp. That of course doesn't make any sense either, but it's an amusing image.

The Compleat Wks of Willm Shkspr (Abridged)

JESS: ...And so much for Scenes One and Two.
So now to the feast of Capulet
Where Romeo is doomed to meet his Juliet.
And where, in a scene of timeless romance,
He'll try to get into Juliet's pants.

(ADAM enters as JULIET, *wearing a wig even sillier than Romeo's. She dances.* ROMEO *enters, sees her, and is immediately smitten.)*

D/ROMEO: "O, she doth teach the torches to burn bright.[20]
Did my heart love 'til now? Forswear it, sight.
For I ne'er saw true beauty 'til this night.
(taking JULIET'S *hand)*
If I profane with my unworthiest hand[21]
This holy shrine, the gentle fine is this:
My lips, two blushing pilgrims ready stand
To smooth that rough touch with a tender kiss.

A/JULIET: Good pilgrim, you do wrong your hands too much,
Which mannerly devotion shows in this;
For saints have hands that pilgrims' hands do touch
And palm to palm is holy palmers' kiss.

---

[20] *'O, she doth teach the torches to burn bright'*; obviously, Romeo's infatuation with Juliet is instant and complete. Post-modern scholars have compared Juliet's effect on Romeo to Bob Marley's effect on the reggae scene in Jamaica. In keeping with this analysis, Juliet in the RSC production wears what appear to be dreadlocks, but is actually a tatty old wig that is never washed or combed because the RSC's costumer is too lazy to be bothered. Thus, in the RSC interpretation, Juliet's untimely death becomes symbolic of Marley's, and Mercutio becomes a metaphor for Peter Tosh. Ayrie.

[21] *'my unworthiest hand'*; most likely a Queen, a Jack, a nine, a four, and a three.

D/ROMEO: Have not saints lips, and holy palmers[22] too?

A/JULIET: Ay, pilgrim. Lips that they must use in prayer.

D/ROMEO: O then, dear saint, let lips do what hands do.

(ADAM has no wish to be kissed and struggles with DANIEL over the following lines.)

A/JULIET: Saints do not move, though grant for prayers' sake.

D/ROMEO: Then move not, while my prayers' effect I take.

A/JULIET: Then from my lips the sin that they have took.

D/ROMEO: Sin from my lips? O trespass sweetly urged. Give me my sin again."

ADAM *(breaking character)*: I don't wanna kiss you, man.

DANIEL: It's in the script.

(ADAM knees DANIEL in the groin. He crumples to the floor in pain.)

A/JULIET: "You kiss by the book." Oh, coming, mother!

(ADAM looks around, curses under his breath. He pulls JESS out of his chair and climbs clumsily onto his shoulders.)

---

[22]*'holy palmers'*; actually 'holey palmers'—coarse, woolen gloves favored by the Roman Catholic clergy of the time which were frequently worn through by excessive groveling.

The Compleat Wks of Willm Shkspr (Abridged)

D/ROMEO: "Is she a Capulet? Ay, so I fear. The more is my unrest."
(breaking character, to ADAM*)* What are you doing?

A/JULIET: The Balcony Scene.[23]

D/ROMEO: "But soft, what light[24] through yonder window breaks?

A/JULIET *(struggling to stay balanced)*:
O Romeo, Romeo, wherefore art thou Romeo?[25]
Deny thy father and refuse thy name,
Or if thou wilt not, be but sworn my love,
And I'll no longer be a Capulet.
What's in a name, anyway? That which we call a nose
By any other name would still smell.
O Romeo, doff thy name,[26] which is no part of thee,
Take all myself. *(Plummets from* JESS' *shoulders.)*

D/ROMEO: I take thee at thy word. Call me but love,[27]

---

[23] *'the Balcony Scene'*; a performance note, supplied by Adam: If Juliet should outweigh Romeo by more than 57 pounds, the 'balcony effect,' as we call it, can be achieved by climbing a tree, suspending yourself by a bungee cord, or, if all else fails, by leaping at least eight feet into the air and hovering there. Under *no circumstances* use an actual balcony.

[24] *'light'*; in this context, obviously a euphemism for 'wind.'

[25] *'wherefore art thou Romeo?'*; perhaps the most widely misconstrued line in all of Shakespeare. The ignorant masses (that's you, humble reader), generally assume 'wherefore' to mean 'where' and believe that Juliet is asking where, in physical space, Romeo is located. In fact, 'wherefore' means 'why.' Juliet is asking him *why* he wastes all his time on his paintings ('Wherefore *art* thou, Romeo?') when he could probably get a real job as an accountant or at least an insurance salesman and a buy a nice late-model carriage to ride in when going out for pizza and espresso and cruising the piazza on Saturday nights.

[26] *'doff thy name'* 'doff': v.t. to misspell (as in: he *doffed* 'lycanthropy' on the vocabulary exam and was chided.)

[27] *'but love'*; 1598 Quarto edition reads, 'butt-love.' In Shakespeare's day, slang for 'homosexual.' See also *Titus Andronicus* (III.ii.197), 'rump ranger,' and *Coriolanus* (V.ii.129) 'rear admiral.'

"Under no cirmumstances use an actual balcony..."
In this series of famous balcony scene portraits, it is obviously the RSC
version (bottom right) which captures the pastoral beauty of the scene.

And I shall be new-baptiz'd.[28] Henceforth
I shall never be Romeo.

A/JULIET: What man art thou?[29] Art thou not Romeo,
And a Montague?

D/ROMEO: Neither, fair maid, if either thee dislike.

A/JULIET: Dost thou love me then? I know thou wilt say aye,
And I will take thy word. Yet if thou swearest,
Thou mayest prove false. O Romeo, if thou dost love,
Pronounce it faithfully.

D/ROMEO: Lady, by yonder blessed moon, I swear—

A/JULIET: O swear not by the moon!

D/ROMEO: What shall I swear by?"

(JULIET points to a woman in the audience.)

Lady, by yonder blessed virgin, I swear—

A/JULIET *(referring to the woman)*: I don't think so. "No,
Do not swear at all. Although I joy in thee,
I have no joy in this contract tonight.

---

[28] *'new-baptized.'*; in earlier performances the line is believed to have been, 'gnu-baptized.' A popular fertility ritual of the late 1500s involved obtaining an exotic animal from a distant land and allowing it to urinate on a virgin. Gnus were among the most popular beasts for the ritual. In fact, the practice became the theme for a highly successful romantic comedy of the time, Ben Jonson's *The Beauty and the Wildebeeste.*

[29] *'What man art thou?'*; again, Juliet is fixated on Romeo's artwork, and wants to know who his male model is. Her suspicions have apparently been aroused by the 'butt-love' reference (see footnote 27).

It is too rash, too sudden, too unadvised,
Too like the lightning, which doth cease to be
Ere one can say it lightens. Sweet, good night.

D/ROMEO: O wilt thou leave me so unsatisfied?[30]

A/JULIET: What satisfaction canst thou have?

D/ROMEO: The exchange of thy love's faithful vows[31] for mine.

A/JULIET: I gave thee mine before thou did'st request it.
Three words, gentle Romeo, and then good night indeed.
If that thy bent of love be honorable,
Thy purpose marriage, send word tomorrow.
Good night, good night; parting is such sweet sorrow—"
Really, it is. *(She exits, blowing a kiss to the love-struck*
ROMEO.*)*

D/ROMEO: "Sleep dwell upon thine eyes, peace in thy breast.
O that I were sleep and peace, so sweet to rest." *(Freezes.)*

JESS: Lo, Romeo did swoon with love;
By Cupid he'd been crippl't;
But Juliet had a loathsome coz
Whose loathsome name was Tybalt.

(ADAM enters as TYBALT, *snarling, carrying two foils.)*

A/TYBALT: "Romeo, the love I bear thee can afford
No better term than this: thou art a villain.[32]

---

[30] *'O wilt thou leave me so unsatisfied?'*; in the 1598 Quarto, 'O Wilt! Thou
leave me so unsatisfied,' signifying a bawdy cameo by basketball legend Wilt
Chamberlain.
[31] *'faithful vows'*; in the 1598 Quarto, 'fateful fluids.'
[32] *'villain'*; in the 1598 Quarto, 'wanker'.

Therefore turn and draw.

D/ROMEO: Tybalt, I do protest, I never injured thee,
But love[33] thee, better than thou canst devise.

A/TYBALT: Thou wretched boy, I am for you!

(TYBALT *throws* ROMEO *a foil.* ROMEO *closes his eyes and extends the blade, neatly impaling the advancing* TYBALT.)

A/TYBALT: O I am slain." (ADAM *bows and exits.*)

(JESS *flips frantically through pages of the book.* DANIEL *is concerned.*)

DANIEL: Now what do we do?

JESS: I don't know. He skipped all this stuff. (*pointing to a place in the book*) Go to here.

DANIEL: Okay. (*Exits.*)

JESS: So...from Tybalt's death onwards, the lovers are cursed
Despite the best efforts of Friar and Nurse;
Their fate pursues them, they can't seem to duck it
And at the end of Act Five, they both kick the bucket.

(JULIET *enters, riding an imaginary horse, humming the 'William Tell Overture.'*)

A/JULIET: "Gallop apace, you fiery-footed steeds,[34]

---

[33]See footnote 27.

[34]*'fiery-footed steeds'*; horse-hotfoots were another cruel pastime of the period, along with bear-baiting, teenage-prostitute scourging, and unedited, four-hour productions of *King Lear*.

And bring in cloudy night immediately.
Come civil night! Come night! Come Romeo,
Thou day in night! Come, gentle night!
Come loving, black-brow'd night!
O night night night night...
Come come come come come!"
(aside to audience) I didn't write it.
"And bring me my Romeo!

(DANIEL enters as the NURSE.)

A/JULIET: O it is my nurse. Now nurse, what news?

D/NURSE: Alack the day, he's gone, he's killed, he's dead!

A/JULIET: Can heaven be so envious?

D/NURSE: Romeo, Romeo! Who ever would have thought it? Romeo!

A/JULIET: What devil art thou to torment me thus? This torture should be roared in dismal hell. Hath Romeo slain himself?

D/NURSE: I saw the wound, I saw it with mine own eyes—God save the mark[35]—here in his manly breast."[36] Men are all dissemblers, they take things apart and reassemble them—I don't know what a dissembler is.

A/JULIET(*accosting a man in the audience*): O no! He's dead! He's

---

[35] '*God save the mark*'; 'mark' was yet another Elizabethan slang term for 'homosexual'; the phrase was later to become 'God save the *queen.*'
[36] '*manly breast*'; the use of oxymoron is fascinating. Daniel is of course portraying a female utilizing one of the most ancient and revered of theatrical conventions: enormous falsies. Hence, as Alexander Pope put it in two centuries ago, 'A mightie cheape Joke.'

gone, he's killed, he's dead, what are you doing tonight?
"O break my heart! Poor bankrupt break at once.
To prison eyes, ne'er look on liberty.
Vile earth to earth resign, end motion here,
And thou and Romeo...go drink a beer.

D/NURSE: O, Tybalt was the best friend I ever had.
That ever I should live to see thee murder'd!

A/JULIET: Is Romeo slaughter'd and is Tybalt dead?
My dear lov'd cousin and my dearer love?
Then dreadful trumpets sound the general doom![37]

D/NURSE: No, Juliet, no! No!
Tybalt is gone and Romeo banished.
Romeo that kill'd Tybalt, he is banished!

A/JULIET: O God! Did Romeo's hand shed Tybalt's blood?

D/NURSE: It did, it did, alas the day it did."

(They sob and scream hysterically, finally pick up mugs and throw water in each other's faces.)

A/JULIET & D/ROMEO *(bowing)*: Thank you.

(DANIEL exits, leaving JULIET alone to assess the situation .)

A/JULIET: Now Romeo lives, whom Tybalt would have slain.
Well, that's good, isn't it?
And Tybalt is dead, who would have killed my husband.
Well, that's good, isn't it?
So why do I feel like poo-poo?

---

[37] *'General Doom™'* is a licensed character of AdventureTime Comics, Inc., all rights reserved.

(DANIEL *enters as* FRIAR LAURENCE.)

O, Friar Laurence! Romeo is banished and Tybalt is slain and...

D/FRIAR: "Juliet, I already know thy grief. Take thou this vial, and this distilled liquor drink thou off.[38] And presently though all thy veins shall run a cold and drowsy humor."

A/JULIET *(Takes bottle and drinks.)*: O, I feel a cold and drowsy humor running through my veins.

D/FRIAR: Told you so.

> (FRIAR *exits.* JULIET *begins to convulse, vomits on several people in the front row, and finally flips over unconscious.* ROMEO *enters. He sees* JULIET *and rushes to her prone body, accidentally stepping on her crotch while doing so.)*

D/ROMEO: "O no! My love, my wife!
Death, that hath suck'd the honey of thy breath,
Hath no power yet upon thy beauty.
O Juliet, why art thou yet so fair?
Shall I believe that unsubstantial death
Is amorous, to keep thee here in the dark
To be his paramour? Here's to my love.
(He drinks from his poison bottle.)
O true apothecary, thy drugs[39] are quick.
Thus, with a kiss, I die...

---

[38] *'this distilled liquor drink thou off'*; the RSC debated intensely about the inclusion of this line, given the saddening abuse of alcohol which ravages our society. However, as the 'distilled liquor' is central to the plot, we include it with this disclaimer: to any children or teenagers who may be reading this book, we wish to affirm our strong commitment to reducing alcoholism in our society. Don't drink. And if you drink, don't drive. Drinking is not cool.
[39] *'drugs'*; drugs, however, are great. Do lots of them.

The Compleat Wks of Willm Shkspr (Abridged)

(This time it is DANIEL *who has no wish to kiss* ADAM. *He struggles with the problem for a moment, takes another swig of poison, and finally kisses him.)*

Thus with a kiss, I die.[40]

*(*ROMEO *dies.* JULIET *wakes up, stretches, scratches her butt, and looks around.)*

A/JULIET: Good morning. Where, O where is my love?

(She sees him lying at her feet and screams.)

"What's this? A cup, closed in my true love's hand?
Poison I see hath been his timeless end. O churl.
Drunk all and left no friendly drop to help me after?
Then I'll be brief. O happy dagger! This is thy sheath."[41]

(She unsheaths ROMEO'S *dagger and does a doubletake: the blade is tiny.)*

---

[40]This editor's lawyer tells him that some impressionable youths might not understand that last footnote was a joke, and that their parents might sue him for many clams when little Johnny bludgeons Aunt Sophie to death with his Stratocaster while under the influence of PCP. He suggests I include a further disclaimer. Although I feel it is out place in a scholarly work such as this, I am legally compelled to say, 'Heh-heh, just kidding, kids. Do whatever Mom and Dad tell you to do. Never question authority. Don't think for yourself, and above all, don't have any fun.'

[41]*'O, happy dagger! This is thy sheath'*; this line again plays on the penis-as-a-sword metaphor (see footnote11). A 'happy dagger' was, of course, an erection, and the sight of the young actor portraying Juliet 'unsheathing' Romeo's would have provoked much general mirth among the groundlings.

That's Romeo for ya.[42]

(JULIET *stabs herself. She screams, but, to her surprise, she does not die. She looks for a wound and can't find one. Finally she realizes that the blade is retractable. This is a cause for much joy. She stabs herself gleefully in the torso and on the crown of the head, delighting in a variety of death noises. Finally, she flings her happy dagger to the ground.)*

"There rust and let me die!" The end! *(Dies.)*

(DANIEL *and* ADAM *rise and bow.* JESS *fetches a guitar from backstage and throws it to* ADAM.)

JESS: Epilogue.

(ADAM *plays theme on guitar* [43] *while* JESS *elucidates the epilogue with gestures.)*

DANIEL: "A glooming peace this morning with it brings;
The sun for sorrow will not show its head;
Go forth and have more talk of these sad things;
Some shall be pardon'd, and some punished;
For never was there a story of more woe
Than this of Juliet and her Romeo."

ALL *(singing)*: And Romeo and Juliet are dead.

(ADAM *plays a rock'n' roll coda on the guitar, ending with all*

---

[42] *'Well, that's Romeo for ya'*; a reference now to the *size* Romeo's genitalia, or alleged lack thereof. If you don't understand the humor of this, you'll be totally lost later in *The Complete Works*, when, in reference to Hamlet, Ophelia complains, 'He comes before me.'

[43] *'theme on guitar'*; this theme can be anything soft, pastoral, and vaguely Elizabethan. As long as it swings.

three doing a synchronized Pete Townshend-style jump[44] *on the last chord.)*

JESS: Thank you, Wembley, and good night!

(Blackout. Lights come back up to reveal DANIEL *alone onstage. The narrator's chair has been struck.)*

DANIEL: Ladies and gentlemen, in preparing this unprecedented 'Complete Works' show, we have encountered this problem: how to make these 400-year-old plays accessible to a modern audience. One popular trend is to take Shakespeare's plays and transpose them into modern settings.[45] We have seen evidence of this with Shakespeare's plays set in such unusual locations as the lunar landscape, Nazi concentration camps, and Cleveland, Ohio. In this vein, Jess has traced the roots of Shakespeare's symbolism in the context of a pre-Nietzschean society through the totality of a jejune circular relationship of form, contrasted with a complete otherness of metaphysical cosmologies, and the ethical mores entrenched in the collective subconscious of an agrarian race.[46] So we now present Shakespeare's first tragedy,

---

[44] *'Pete Townshend-style jump'*; Jess recalls, 'In a fascinating experiment, Adam once attempted to smash a guitar onstage à la Townshend (lead guitar player for the seminal rock band, The Who). Interestingly enough, where Mr. Townshend's guitar-smashing provokes screaming pubescent girls to throw themselves at him in a frenzy of sexual abandonment, the same action performed by a Shakespeare-an actor elicited only stunned silence and some rather nasty splinters.'

[45] *'transpose them into modern settings'*; a practice which, quite frankly, gets this editor's panties in a bunch. Whether it's a production of Shakespeare or Sophocles, today's theater-goer must live in dread of walking into a theater and discovering that some classic work has been given a modernized, socially relevant setting. Oedipus gouges his eyes with a spoon at a 1950's malt shop; Macbeth napalms Banquo in Viet Nam, Julius Caesar dies in Dallas in 1963. More and more, American theater is coming to resemble a season of *Quantum Leap*. Oooo, it makes me *angry*!

[46] *'Ladies and gentlemen...agrarian race'*; don't bother reading that sentence over again. It's covering a costume change and is absolutely meaningless.

Act One

'Titus Andronicus,' as a cooking show.

(JESS enters as TITUS ANDRONICUS, *wearing an apron and carrying a large butcher's knife. He is somewhat reminiscent of Julia Child.)*

J/TITUS: Good evening, everyone! Good evening, gore-mets, and welcome to 'Roman Meals.' I'm your host, Titus Androgynous. Now, when you've had a long day—your left hand chopped off, your sons murdered, your daughter raped, her tongue cut out, and both her hands chopped off—well, the last thing you want to do is cook. Unless, of course, you cook the rapist and serve him to his mother at a dinner party! My daughter Lavinia and I will show you how.

(ADAM enters as LAVINIA, *clutching a large mixing bowl held between her stumps, pushing DANIEL as the* RAPIST *in front of her.)*

Good evening, Lavinia!

A/LAVINIA: Ood ebeie, mubba.[47]

---

[47] *'Ood ebeie, mubba'*; it is fairly well accepted among scholars that what Lavinia *intends* to say in this line is:

> My bloody mater, vouchsafe our revenge
> Upon this vile and decrepit worm
> Shall rock the heavens and unleash the clouds
> To pour upon his head this horrid justice!

However, because her tongue has been chopped out, what she actually says is:

> Ood ebeie, mubba.

In creating the dialogue for the tongueless Lavinia, the RSC conducted extensive research into an uncharted branch of linguistic study: tongueless speech. After removing the tongues of a carefully monitored study group of white mice, the RSC realized that the mice couldn't talk to begin with. But the experiment was so much fun they hope to continue their work, perhaps on a more tightly focused study group—say, for example, talk radio personality Rush Limbaugh.

Titus Andronicus
"...Your daughter raped, her tongue cut out, and both her hands chopped off..."
Yeah, but look at how she was dressed, Your Honor—she was asking *for it!*

J/TITUS: And how are we feeling today?

A/LAVINIA: Ot so ood, mubba. I ot my ongue tsopped off.

J/TITUS: I know. It's a pisser, isn't it? But we'll get our revenge, won't we?
"Now hark, villain. I will grind your bones to dust,
And of your blood and it I'll make a paste;
And of the paste a coffin I will rear
And make a pasty of your shameful head.
Come, Lavinia, receive the blood."
First of all, we want to make a nice, clean incision from carotid artery to jugular vein *(slicing* RAPIST'S *throat)*, like so.

RAPIST: Aaaaargh!

A/LAVINIA: Yecch. That's weally gwoss, mubba.

J/TITUS: Be sure to use a big bowl for this because the human body has about four quarts of blood in it! "And when that he is dead," which should be...

(LAVINIA has dragged the RAPIST'S *body to the doorway, where we see the butcher's knife rise and fall.* RAPIST'S *body convulses once, and then is dragged away.)*

...right about now, "let me go grind his bones to powder small
And with this hateful liquor[48] temper it;
And in that paste let his vile head be baked..."[49]

---

[48] *'hateful liquor'*; most scholars, this editor included, are confused by the notion of unpleasant alcoholic beverages.

[49] *'head be baked'*; baking human heads into meat pies was in fact a contemporary English, not a Roman, practice. Although the culinary technique was discontinued in the mid-1980s, it has left a linguistic mark: even today, we like to call English people 'pasty-faced.'

The Compleat Wks of Willm Shkspr (Abridged)

At about 350 degrees. And 40 minutes later, you have the loveliest human head pie...

(LAVINIA re-enters with a truly disgusting pie, prepared earlier.)

...fit to serve to a king *(pulling a severed hand from the pie)*, with ladyfingers for dessert! Now, who will be the first to try this delicious taste treat?

(TITUS and LAVINIA offer the pie to a COUPLE in the audience.)

"Welcome, gracious lord. Welcome, dread queen.
Will't please you eat? Will't please you feed?"
It's finger-lickin' good!

(JESS and ADAM are excited by the clever line. They try to give each other a high-five, but since neither has a hand, it is a miserable failure.)

Well, we're just about out of time, everyone. Thanks for tuning in, and be sure to watch next week, when our guest chef, Timon of Athens, will teach us how to make ratatouille out of our special guests, the Merry Wives of Windsor! Until then...

J/TITUS AND A/LAVINIA: Bone appètit![50]

(They exit. A moment later, DANIEL enters.)

---

[50] *'bone appètit'*; this is widely acknowledged by modern scholars to be absolutely the worst joke in the entire show.

DANIEL: I hope no one was too offended by 'Titus Andronicus.'
Shakespeare as a young writer seems to have gone through an
early blood and guts period. No doubt, if he were alive today
he'd be in Hollywood working on 'Titus Andronicus IX—Just
Desserts.' But we shall now move on to explore the genius
evident in Shakespeare's more mature[51] plays, as we present his
dark and brooding tragedy, 'Othello, the Moor of Venice.'

*(DANIEL exits. ADAM enters as OTHELLO, with plastic boats
on a string draped around his neck.)*

A/OTHELLO: "Speak of me as I am; let nothing extenuate
Of one who loved not wisely, but too well:"
For never was there a story of more woe
Than this of Othello and his Desdemono
(He stabs himself with a tugboat.)
O, Desi!
(He dies amid a clatter of plastic boats.)

*(DANIEL and JESS watch from the doorway in distress. They
confer briefly, then enter.)*

DANIEL *(to the light booth)*: Bob, can we have some lights
please?[52] We left Adam on his own to research this play. He
must have looked up 'Moor' in the dictionary and thought it was
a place where you tie up boats.

---

[51] *'mature'*; containing nudity.

[52] *'Bob'*; research has proven that 44% of all theater dimmer-board operators, as
well as audience members selected at random, are named 'Bob.' After many
weeks of touring, the RSC decided it was easier to automatically call the person
in the booth 'Bob' with the assumption that almost half the time they were
correct. (See also page 85.)

JESS: Which, in this context, is totally pea-brained. In the sixteenth century the word 'moor'[53] referred to a black person.

ADAM: Oh. I feel like such a dork.[54] *(He exits.)*

JESS: Now, ladies and gentlemen, we obviously have a little bit of a problem in performing 'Othello,' because the part is written for a black man, and we're obviously not, I mean...

JESS AND DANIEL *(ad lib)*: ...we don't really have the physical characteristics necessary to portray...yeah, we're really Southern California white trash surfer dude types... well...

JESS AND DANIEL *(simultaneously)*: We're honkies...

JESS: ...basically, is what we are. So the bottom line here is that due to physical limitations, we are unable to perform 'Othello, the Moor of Venice,' so we'll move on to...

(ADAM enters, sans boats.)

ADAM: Hey you guys, come on. We can do it. Just because we're white doesn't mean we can't do 'Othello.' I got an idea, just kinda join in...

---

[53] *'moor'*; it has since been discovered that the historical Othello's first name was Les; hence the expression 'Les is Moor.'

[54] *'I feel like such a dork'*; further research has shown that 'Moor,' in Shakespearean context, *does* refer to boats, and that *Othello* was originally referred to as 'Shakespeare's Nautical Play.' Therefore, Adam was correct in his analysis of the play, and his co-authors owe him an apology. It should also be noted that in the mid-1600's, rural communities were performing *Othello* with a bovine bias, referring to him as 'the Moo-er of Venice.' Fortunately, these performances were the exception rather than the rule.

(He begins snapping his fingers in a rap[55] beat.)

Here's the story of a brother by the name of Othello
He liked white women and he liked green Jello

JESS *(catching on quickly)*: Oh, yeah, yeah. Uh...
And a punk named Iago who made hisself a menace
'Cos he didn't like Othello, the Moor of Venice.

ADAM: Now Othello got married to Des-demona,

JESS: But he took off for the wars and he left her alone-a.

ADAM: It was a moan-a

JESS: A groan-a

ADAM AND JESS: He left her alone-a.

DANIEL *(finally catching on and joining in)*:
He didn't write a letter and he didn't telephone-a!

(They all get into it, stomping and clapping to the beat.[56])

Desdemona, she was faithful, she was chastity-tight
She was the daughter of a duke

---

[55] *'rap'*; excellent examples of the 'rap' genre can be found in the recordings of Ice Cube and The Disposable Heroes of HipHoprisy. It should be noted at this point that the authors fully realize how trite and overused rapping is as a way to show youth, vivacity and attitude. Even in 1989, when Jess and Adam first penned the piece in a late-night hotel room debauch in Honolulu, rap was overdone. And yet, *Rap Othello* is one of the most consistently crowd-pleasing sections of the show. I guess what we're saying here is that the RSC's audiences are pretty dumb, but the performers are more than willing to compromise their artistic integrity and sink to their level. Such is the magic of theater.

[56] *'beat'* is here used loosely, as the performers are all extremely white.

ADAM: Yeah she was totally white.
But Iago had a plan that was clever and slick
He was crafty

DANIEL: He was sly

JESS: He was sort of a dick.

ADAM: He say 'I'm gonna shaft the Moor.'

DANIEL: How you gonna do it?

DANIEL AND JESS: Tell us!

ADAM: Well I know his tragic flaw is that he's

ALL: Too damn jealous!

ADAM: I need a dupe
I need a dope
I need a kind of a shmoe...

JESS: So he find a chump sucker by the name o' Cassio.

DANIEL: And he plants on him Desdemona's handkerchief,

ADAM: So Othello gets to wonderin just maybe if...
While he been out fightin

DANIEL AND ADAM: Commandin an army

JESS: Are Desi and Cass playin hide the salami?
Sa-sa-sa-salam
Salaaammii![57]

---

[57] *'Salaaammii!'*; a nod by the performers to the plays of Oscar Wilde.

DANIEL: So he come back home an stick a pillow in her face

JESS: Kills her, and soliloquizes 'bout his disgrace.

ADAM: But there's Emilia at the door

JESS: Who we met in Act Four

DANIEL: Who say, 'You big dummy, she weren't no whore. She was

ALL: Pure

DANIEL: She was

ALL: Clean

DANIEL: She was

ALL: Virginal, too,
So why'd you have to go and make her face turn blue?

ADAM: It's true

DANIEL: It's you

ADAM AND DANIEL: Now what you gonna do?'

ADAM: And Othello say:

JESS: 'Yo, this is gettin pretty scary.'

DANIEL: So he pulled out his blade and committed hari-kari.

The Compleat Wks of Willm Shkspr (Abridged)

ADAM: Iago got caught, but he prob'ly copped a plea,

JESS: Loaded up his bags,

DANIEL: And moved to Beverly...

ALL: ...Hills, that is.

(Bows and elaborate handshakes all round.)

JESS AND ADAM *(fists held high in a black power salute)*: Africa![58]

DANIEL: Why don't we take a break from all this heavy tragedy and move on to the Comedies for awhile?

ADAM AND JESS: Comedies! Yeah, great. Comedies, okay. *(They exit.)*

DANIEL: Now, when it came to the Comedies, Shakespeare was a genius at borrowing and adapting plot devices from different theatrical traditions.

(JESS re-enters, wearing a tailcoat and carrying another which he gives to DANIEL.)

JESS: That's right. These influences include the Roman plays of Plautus and Terence, Ovid's 'Metamorphoses,'[59] which are hysterically funny—NOT—as well as the rich Italian tradition of Commedia Dell'Arte.

---

[58] *'Africa'*; a large continent south of Italy and to the right of Brazil.

[59] *'Metamorphoses'*; Jess is very proud of the fact that he has read Ovid's *Metamorphoses* in the original Latin, although he's just guessing about the Plautus and Terence stuff. When asked if he isn't really just a sanctimonious, supercilious, egghead classical scholar snob, Jess quickly replied in flawless Latin, *'Futue te impsum et caballum tuum.'* (Literally, 'Screw you and the horse you rode in on.')

(ADAM re-enters, wearing a tailcoat and carrying scripts, which he distributes to DANIEL and JESS.)

ADAM: Yeah. Basically, Shakespeare stole everything he ever wrote.

JESS: 'Stole' is kinda strong, dude. 'Distilled,' maybe.

ADAM: Well, then he 'distilled' the three or four funniest gimmicks of his time, and then he milked them into sixteen plays.

DANIEL: You see, essentially Shakespeare was a formula writer. Once he found a device that worked, he used it...

ALL: Over and over and over again.

DANIEL: So, Mr. Shakespeare, the question we have is this:

ALL: Why did you write sixteen comedies when you could have written just one?

JESS: In answer to this question, we have taken the liberty of condensing all sixteen of Shakespeare's comedies into a single play, which we have entitled 'The Comedy of Two Well-Measured Gentlemen Lost in the Merry Wives of Venice on a Midsummer's Twelfth Night in Winter.'

ADAM: Or...

DANIEL: 'Cymbeline Taming Pericles the Merchant in the Tempest of Love As Much As You Like It For Nothing.'

ADAM: Or...

The Compleat Wks of Willm Shkspr (Abridged)

ALL: 'The Love Boat Goes to Verona.'

(All pivot and march upstage. Blackout . In the blackout, we hear:)

ADAM: Comedy?

JESS: Comedy.

DANIEL: Comedy.

(Lights come up to reveal all three actors, each in a pool of light and wearing tailcoats and comedy headgear. DANIEL wears goggles; ADAM wears floppy bug antennae and a clown nose; JESS wears a pair of Groucho Marx-funny-nose-and-glasses.)

DANIEL: Act One. A Spanish duke swears an oath of celibacy and turns the rule of his kingdom over to his sadistic and tyrannical twin brother. He learns some fantastical feats of magic and sets sail for the Golden Age of Greece, along with his daughters, three beautiful and virginal sets of identical twins. While rounding the heel of Italy,[60] the duke's ship is caught in a terrible tempest which, in its fury, casts the duke up on a desert island, along with the loveliest and most virginal of his daughters, who stumbles into a cave, where she is molested by a creature who is either a man or a fish or both.[61]

ADAM: Act Two. The long-lost children of the duke's brother, also coincidentally three sets of identical twins, have just arrived in Italy. Though still possessed of an inner nobility, they are

---

[60] *'Italy'*; a small country just north of Africa and left of China. Shaped like a boot.

[61] *'man or a fish or both'*; other wonders of the animal kingdom include: the bombardier beetle, which emits explosive flatulence in self-defense; the platypus; Mr. Ed; and the banana slug, state mollusk of California.

ragged, destitute, penniless, flea-infested shadows of the men they once were, and in the utmost extremity, are forced to borrow money from an old Jew, who deceives them into putting down their brains as collateral on the loan. Meanwhile, the six brothers fall in love with six Italian sisters, three of whom are contentious, sharp-tonged little shrews, while the other three are submissive, airheaded little bimbos.

JESS: Act Three. The shipwrecked identical daughters of the duke wash up on the shores of Italy, disguise themselves as men, and become pages to the shrews, and matchmakers to the duke's brother's sons. They lead all the lovers into a nearby forest, where, on a midsummer's night, a bunch of mischievous fairies squeeze the aphroditic juice of a hermaphroditic flower in the shrews' eyes, causing them to fall in love with their own pages, who in turn have fallen in love with the duke's brother's sons, while the 'Queen' of the 'fairies' seduces a jackass, and they all have a lovely bisexual animalistic orgy.

ALL: Act Four!

DANIEL: The elderly fathers of the Italian sisters, finding their daughters missing, dispatch messages to the pages, telling them to kill any man in the vicinity.

ADAM: However, unable to find men in the forest, the faithful messengers, in a final, misguided act of loyalty, deliver the messages to each other and kill themselves.

JESS: Meanwhile, the fish-creature and the duke arrive in the forest disguised as Russians, and for no apparent reason, perform a two-man underwater version of 'Uncle Vanya.'

ALL: Act Five!

The Compleat Wks of Willm Shkspr (Abridged)

A Lovely Bisexual Animalistic Orgy

DANIEL: The duke commands the fairies to right their wrongs.

ADAM: The pages and the bimbos get into a knock-down drag-out fight in the mud...

JESS: During which the pages' clothes get ripped off, revealing female genitalia!

DANIEL: The duke recognizes his daughters!

ADAM: The duke's brother's sons recognize their uncle...

JESS: One of the bimbos grows up to be Vanna White...

DANIEL: And they all get married and go out to dinner.

ADAM: Except for a minor character in the second act who gets eaten by a bear, and the duke's brother's sons who, unable to pay back the old Jew, give themselves lobotomies.

ALL: And they all live happily ever after.[62]

(All bow. DANIEL and JESS exit.)

ADAM: We now move on to the rest of Shakespeare's tragedies, because basically we've found that the Comedies aren't half as funny as the Tragedies. Take for example, Shakespeare's Scottish Play, 'Mac—

(JESS and DANIEL re-enter, frantically.)

---

[62] *'happily ever after'*; there is really nothing further of interest to say about the Comedies. If the authors hadn't foolishly titled the show *The Complete Works of William Shakespeare* before they wrote it, they would have skipped them altogether.

The Compleat Wks of Willm Shkspr (Abridged)

JESS AND DANIEL *(ad lib)*: Sssshhh![63] Don't talk about it in here!

ADAM: Oh, gosh, sorry. I forgot.

ALL *(whispering to audience)*: Which you're really not supposed to talk about in a theater unless you're performing it, because it's cursed. *(leaping into front row, loudly)* Booga, booga, booga![64]

(JESS and ADAM exit.)

DANIEL: Fortunately, however, we of the Reduced Shakespeare Company not only perform an abbreviated version of 'Macbeth—'

---

[63] *'Sssshhh!'*; the RSC here addresses the superstition that uttering the name of this allegedly accursed play is bad luck. Those who flaunt the curse have been known to die mysteriously, go bankrupt, or suffer through agonizing careers as low-paid actors in a traveling theater troupe.

[64] *'Booga, booga, booga'*; one of the most provocative of all subjects in early Shakespearean scholarship, and later in comic theory. The phrase first appears in an entry in Samuel Pepys' diary in 1598: 'Saw Shaksper's most excellente *Henry VI* today. King Edward did rallye his ryght noble lords to battle, wi' the crye,

> Edward dares, and leads the way.
> Lords, to the field; Saint George and victory,
> Booga, booga, booga!'

The device has developed in an unbroken line since then, although during the reign of Queen Victoria the phrase was modified to 'ooga, ooga, ooga;' apparently the letter B was too overtly sexual for the Victorian sensibility, shaped as it was like the very Buttocks of the Queen in question, and appearing in many other words directly related to sexual apparatus, such as 'breasts,' 'bottom,' 'bollocks,' and 'bring me the dildo please, dear.' In modern comic usage, the phrase is often accompanied by a flapping of the cheeks and jowls and repeated 'b' sounds, although even within the RSC there is dissent as to whether the flapping b's should precede or follow the 'Booga, booga, booga.' This editor expresses no preference; I suggest that you, humble reader, try both approaches in the bathroom mirror, so you can see for yourself how truly degrading comic acting can be.

A lovely rendering of Macbeth, *a play foolishly believed to be "cursed" by the simple-minded and superstitious masses.*

(ADAM re-enters with DANIEL'S witch costume, trips over his own feet and falls flat on his face.)

But, after much thorough research, we are able to do so...

DANIEL AND ADAM: ...in perfect Scottish accents!

(DANIEL dons the costume and becomes the WITCH as ADAM exits.)

D/WITCH: "Double, double,[65] toil and trouble.

(JESS enters as MACBETH, with a sword. In nearly impenetrable Scottish accents:)

J/MACBETH: Stay, ye imperrrfect macspeaker. Mactell me macmore.

D/WITCH: Macbeth, Macbeth, beware Macduff.
None of woman born shall harm Macbeth
Till Birnam Wood come to Dunsinane, don't ye know.

(WITCH exits. ADAM enters as MACDUFF, hiding behind a twig.)

---

[65] *'Double, double'*; Higgins has hypothesized (*Shakespeare Quarterly*, Summer of '42) that the witches in this famous scene are not, in fact, stirring a caldron, but shooting craps.

J/MACBETH: O, that's dead great. Then macwhat macneed macI macfear of Macduff?

(MACDUFF throws down his disguise, wields his sword and throws a two-fingered gesture at MACBETH)

A/MACDUFF: See you, Jimmy, and know
That I was from my mother's womb untimely ripped!"
What d'ye think about that?

J/MACBETH: It's bloody disgusting. Lay on, ye great haggis-face.

(They fence.)

A/MACDUFF: Ah, Macbeth! Ye killed my wife, ye murdered my babies, ye shat in my stew.

J/MACBETH: Och! I didnae!

A/MACDUFF: O, ay ye did. I had t' throw half of it away.

*(MACDUFF chases MACBETH offstage. Backstage,
MACBETH'S scream is abruptly cut off. MACDUFF re-enters
carrying a severed head.)*

A/MACDUFF: Behold where lies the usurper's cursed head.
Macbeth, yer arse is out the windie.
(Dropkicks the head into the audience.) And know,
That never was there a story of blood and death
Than this, o' Mr. and Mrs. Macbeth.[66] Thankee. *(Exits.)*

---

[66]The RSC *Macbeth* plays on nearly every demeaning Scottish stereotype extant in contemporary society. First, that they unnecessarily trill their R's; second, that they call each other names based on the less appetizing aspects of Scottish cuisine; and third, that all Scots are tight-fisted penny-pinching misers. In fact, only two major stereotypes have been omitted: that Scottish people look ridiculous in kilts (see footnote regarding plaid, footnote 10) and that they like to run around saying, 'Captin, the engines canna take any more.'

The Compleat Wks of Willm Shkspr (Abridged)

(JESS enters.)

JESS: Meanwhile, Julius Caesar[67] was a much-beloved tyrant.

(ADAM enters.)

ADAM AND JESS: All hail, Julius Caesar!

(DANIEL enters as JULIUS CAESAR, wearing a laurel wreath.)

D/CAESAR: Hail, citizens!

JESS: Who was warned by a soothsayer...

(ADAM pulls his shirt over his head and becomes the SOOTHSAYER.)

A/SOOTHSAYER: "Beware the Ides of March."

JESS: The great Caesar, however, chose to ignore the warning.

D/CAESAR: What the hell are the Ides of March?

A/SOOTHSAYER: The 15th of March.

D/CAESAR: Why, that's today.

---

[67]*'Meanwhile, Julius Caesar'*; those who have wondered aloud (and they are many) about this seemingly odd transition from *Macbeth* to *Julius Caesar* have missed an essential proof of the RSC genius. Obviously, the 'I was from my mother's womb untimely ripp'd' scene in *Macbeth* and the tragic tale of Rome's great Emperor both belong here, in the *Caesarian Section* of the show.

(JESS and ADAM stab him repeatedly. He falls. ADAM exits.)

D/CAESAR: "Et tu, Brute?[68]

(CAESAR dies. JESS becomes MARK ANTONY, orating over the body.)

J/ANTONY: Friends, Romans, countrymen, lend me your ears. I come to bury Caesar," so bury him, and let's get on to my play, 'Antony...

(ADAM enters as CLEOPATRA, wearing a wig and clutching a rubber snake.)

---

[68] *'Et tu, Brute?'*; Shakespeare, according to Ben Jonson, knew 'little Latin and less Greek,' and it shows here. Jess' research into Plutarch's *Lives* indicates that the full dialogue between Caesar and Brutus probably went something like this:

LATIN	ENGLISH TRANSLATION
BRU: In tempore praeterito plus quam perfecto de te mox dicent, Caesare!	BRU: People will soon have to refer to you in the past pluperfect tense, Caesar!
CAE: Di! Ecce hora! Uxor mea me necabit. Abeo!	CAE: Golly, look at the time! My wife will kill me. I'm outta here!
BRU: Ecce! Spiritus Elvis!	BRU: Look! The ghost of Elvis!
CAE: Ubi?	CAE: Where?
(Caesar caeduntur)	*(Caesar is stabbed)*
CAE: Et tu, Brute? Ad domum adligaris, et nullam ultravisionem spectabis per septem dies! Subito minime valeo. O, obesa cantavit!	CAE: Even you, Brutus? You're grounded, and no television for a week. Suddenly, I don't feel so good. O, the fat lady has sung!
(Mortuus est.)	*(Dies.)*

The Compleat Wks of Willm Shkspr (Abridged)

A/CLEOPATRA: ...and Cleopatra!' Is this an asp I see before me?

(CLEOPATRA *applies the snake to her breast, and immediately vomits on several people in the front row.*)[69]

JESS AND DANIEL: Whoa, Adam! No! Stop!

ADAM: What?

DANIEL: You have this bizarre notion that all of Shakespeare's tragic heroines wear really ugly wigs and vomit on people before they die.

ADAM: Well...don't they?

JESS: No, no—get a clue, man. 'Antony and Cleopatra' is not a Pepto-Bismol commercial. It's a romantic thriller about a geopolitical power struggle between Egypt and Rome.

ADAM: Oh, it's one of Shakespeare's geopolitical plays? Wow, if I'd known that I'd never have screwed around with it, 'cause Shakespeare's geopolitical work is my favorite stuff. It's like, the themes he wrote about four hundred years ago are still relevant today. Like what was that one he wrote about how nuclear energy affected the Soviet Union?

JESS: Adam, Shakespeare never wrote anything about the Soviet Union.

---

[69] *'vomits on several people'*; actually, here as elsewhere, Adam only *pretends* to vomit on several people in the front row. Vomiting is illegal in most theaters, except during productions of *Joseph and the Amazing Technicolor Dreamcoat*.

ADAM: Yeah, he totally did. It was called 'Chernobyl Kinsmen'[70] and it was intense...[71]

DANIEL: Adam, what are you talking about?

ADAM: 'Chernobyl Kinsmen,' It was recently attributed—

DANIEL: No, Adam. Shakespeare wrote a play called 'Two Noble Kinsmen.'

JESS: Not 'Chernobyl Kinsmen!'

DANIEL: 'Two Noble Kinsmen.'

ADAM: Oh. What's 'Two Noble Kinsmen' about?

JESS: It's about a girl who goes insane with the fear that her boyfriend is going to be eaten by wolves and her father hanged.

ADAM: And is there anything in it about Boris Yeltsin?

JESS AND DANIEL: No.

ADAM: Well, I've never even heard of that play.

JESS: I'm not surprised you haven't heard of it, because it's not actually...hmm. Maybe I should explain. *(turning to the audience)* Ladies and gentlemen, 'Two Noble Kinsmen' actually falls into the category of Shakespeare's plays which scholars refer to as 'The Apocrypha,' or in some scholarly circles, 'The

---

[70] *'Chernobyl Kinsmen'*; or, *The Nuclear Winter's Tale*.

[71] *'it was intense...'*; at this point Adam very often rambles for a minute or more about current events, weaving a conspiratorial tale of nuclear fallout, corrupt politicians, debauched evangelists and/or whatever bug he has up his butt at the time.

Obscure Plays,' or 'The Lesser Plays,' or simply, 'The Bad Plays.'[72] And yet, not all of The Apocrypha are completely without merit. In fact, one of them, 'Troilus and Cressida,' is hardly crap at all. *(He's becoming excited with the breadth of his own scholarly achievement now.)* I actually discuss it at some length in my soon-to-be-released book about Shakespeare, entitled 'I Love My Willy,' which I'd like to whip out for you now *(reaching into his pants and extracting...a manuscript).* I was thinking that maybe tonight we could do a kind of a quick improvised version of 'Troilus and Cressida'[73] based on this chapter.

DANIEL: Yeah! We could do an interpretive dance/performance art version!

ADAM: Oh, I love performance art. It's so... *(searching for the word)* ...pretentious! We could use 'Troilus and Cressida' as a jumping-off point to explore deeper themes like the transient nature of life and the mythology involved in the arising and dissipation of forms.

DANIEL: Yeah, get some props!

JESS: Now wait just a minute. I was actually thinking of a straightforward, scholarly approach—

ADAM: Naw, screw that. *(He exits.)*

---

[72] *'The Bad Plays'*; among the other 'Apocrypha' are many which didn't make it into the standard accepted list of Shakespeare's *Complete Works*. These include the tragedies *Sir Thomas More* and *A Yorkshire Tale,* as well as comedies such as *Ye Odd Couple* and early musicals such as *Ye Cats, Ye Miserables,* and *Joseph and Ye Amazing Technicolor Dreamdoublet.*

[73] *'Troilus and Cressida'*; in Japan, this play is well-known and often-revived, although the title is generally altered, for commercial reasons, to *Toyota and Cressida.*

DANIEL: Go ahead and read. *(He poses.)*

JESS: Well, okay. 'Troilus and Cressida' was written in 1603, published in quarto in 1604, and appears in the First Folio, although this version is some 166 lines longer than the second quarto edition of 1645, in which appears the famous "chihuahua" scene...

> *(DANIEL performs an awkward dance-mime as ADAM re-enters, first with an inflatable dinosaur and then with a battery-operated Godzilla[74] that walks and roars. DANIEL and JESS stare at the machine, and then at ADAM, until he turns it off and exits like a wounded puppy dog, taking his toy with him.)*

JESS: Ladies and gentlemen, my book has nothing to do with Godzilla.[75] It discusses the possibility that Shakespeare's plays were actually written by Elvis Presley.[76] I think it's groundbreaking work, you see he was abducted by aliens and entered a time-warp—

DANIEL: Wait a minute. Isn't there something in there about the plot?

> *(ADAM re-enters with a crown.)*

JESS: Plot? Of course I cover the plot. What kind of scholar do you think I am? I cover the plot in depth in the footnote on page

---

[74] *'battery-operated Godzilla'*; to the authors' knowledge, the battery operated Godzilla, a.k.a. 'Rex,' (so named to avoid copyright infringement) can only be found at: the Dinosaur Store, in Lyme Regis, England; Heathrow International Airport, Terminal One; and Pier 39, San Francisco. NOTE: When playing in Tokyo, it's probably best to cut Godzilla from the show, as the locals are known to respond with mindless and ineffectual panic.

[75] *'nothing to do with Godzilla'*; here, Jess misses the essential connection of Shakespeare to Godzilla, which is...um...oh, forget it.

[76] *'Elvis Presley'*; a primitive forerunner of Elvis Costello.

twenty-nine. *(reading)* 'Troilus, youngest son of Priam, King of Troy...'

ADAM: Okay, you be Troilus and you *(crowning JESS)* be the King.

JESS: Okay, great. '...loves Cressida...'

(JESS and DANIEL look at ADAM.)

ADAM: I'll get the wig. *(ADAM exits, fetches the wig and re-enters.)*

JESS: '...and has arranged with her uncle Pandarus for a meeting. Although she feigns indifference, she is attracted to him...'

ADAM: I have to feign indifference?!

JESS: Yeah! '...meanwhile, Agamemnon,[77] the Greek commander, has surrounded the Trojans—'[78]

ADAM AND DANIEL: Agamemnon?!? Jess, this is boring, boring boring!

DANIEL: This is the kind of stuff that kids hate to study in school because it's so boring.

ADAM: Yeah, like as soon as you said 'Agamemnon,' I was asleep. No, I'm sorry *(to audience)* but when I heard we were coming to (insert name of town here), I told these guys, 'I will NOT do dry,

---

[77] *'Agamemnon'*; an anglicized version of the original Greek name œ∑æΩ¥œæΩ∂, sometimes translated "King of the People Who Will Dork Anything That Moves."

[78] *'Trojans'*; as opposed to the fun-loving Greeks, the Trojans of the earliest Greek myths (that is, before Homer adapted them to his own purposes in the *Iliad*) were an ascetic society of men and women who dedicated their lives to safe sex. Legend had it they were so successful they quickly died out as a race.

boring...vomitless Shakespeare for these people, 'cause it'll just turn you off. I mean, that's what happened to me. When I was a kid I used to sit there in class,[79] while we were supposed to be studying Shakespeare, and I'd be looking out the window at all the kids playing ball, and I'd be thinking to myself, 'Why can't this Shakespeare stuff be more like sports?'

JESS: Sports?

DANIEL: How do you mean?

ADAM: Well, sports are visceral, they're exciting to watch. I mean, take the histories, for example. With all those kings and queens killing each other off, and the throne passing from one generation to the next. It's exactly like playing football, but you do it with a crown.

JESS: Hey, they are kinda similar, aren't they?

DANIEL: Yeah, I can see that. Okay, line 'em up. Let's get macho!

(They line up in a three-man football formation. Then, like a quarterback calling signals:)

Twenty-five!...Forty-two...Richard the Third...Henry the Fifth, Part One! Two! Three...

ALL: HUP!

---

[79] *'sit there in class'*; when contacted to confirm this anecdote, Adam's fourth-grade teacher, Mrs. Peachum, replied, 'Sit there, HAH! He used to climb on top of the coat closet and try to pee on the girls. I had to strap him into his seat with gaffer's tape on a daily basis! He made my life a living hell, the little @#%!'

The Compleat Wks of Willm Shkspr (Abridged)

JESS *(like a football announcer)*: ...and the crown is snapped to Richard the Second, that well-spoken fourteenth-century monarch. He's fading back to pass, looking for an heir downfield, but there's a heavy rush from King John. *(JESS, as KING JOHN, stabs DANIEL.)*

D/RICHARD II: "My gross flesh sinks downwards!"

JESS: The crown is in the air, and Henry the Sixth comes up with it!

A/HENRY VI: Victory is mine!

DANIEL *(announcer)*: But he's hit immediately by King John, that rarely performed player from the twelfth century, and he's down.

(JESS Begins stabbing the fallen HENRY VI repeatedly.)

Ooh, he's killin' him out there! This could be the end of the War of the Roses cycle!

ADAM *(announcer)*: King John is in the clear...

J/KING JOHN: "My soul hath elbow room!"

ADAM: He's at the forty, the thirty, the twenty—he's poisoned on the ten yard line! *(JESS exits.)* Looks like he's out for the game. Replacing him now is number seventy-two, King Lear.

D/LEAR: "Divide we our kingdom in three." Cordelia, you go long...

(JESS re-enters, throws a penalty marker and whistles play dead.)

ADAM: A penalty marker is down.

(JESS makes a hand signal and points at LEAR.)

Fictional character on the field. Lear is disqualified, and he's not happy about it.

D/LEAR: Puckey![80]

ADAM: Lining up now is that father-son team of Henry the Fourth and Prince Hal. Center snaps to the quarterback...quarterback gives to the hunchback. It looks like Richard the Third's limp is giving him trouble.

D/RICHARD III: "A horse, a horse! My kingdom for a horse!"[81]

(A massive crunch as RICHARD III goes down, and JESS and the DUMMY pile on top.)

ADAM: There's a pile-up on the field.

DANIEL *(announcer)*: FUM-BLE!!! And Henry the Eighth comes up with it. He's at the twenty, the fifteen, the ten...He stops at the five to chop off his wife's head...TOUCHDOWN for the Red Rose! Oh, my! You gotta believe this is the beginning of a Tudor Dynasty!

---

[80] *'Fictional character...Puckey!'*; quite possibly the funniest joke in the entire show. It contains all the elements necessary in a truly first-class jape, to wit: temporal juxtaposition, that is, the incongruity of a Shakespearean character playing football; inside reference, as those who know their Shakespeare know that *King Lear* is in fact accounted a tragedy and that there is no historical record of his existence; and finally, an excellent nonsense word, 'puckey,' which contains the two funniest letters in the English language, 'p' and 'k.' In this passage, the boys have nearly attained the genius of the Bard himself.

[81] *'A horse, a horse, my kingdom for a horse'*; one of the most famous lines in all of Shakespeare, first made popular by Catherine the Great late one lonely night in St. Petersburg.

J & A/CHEERLEADERS: Henry the Fifth, Richard the Third, Di is a babe and Charles a turd![82] Goooo, FERGIE![83]

(DANIEL and JESS congratulate each other as ADAM clambers into the audience.)

ADAM: Can I have some house lights please? *(to an audience member)* Can I borrow your program for a sec?

DANIEL: What are you doing?

ADAM: I just want to check the list of plays. I think we might have done 'em all already.

JESS: Really?

ADAM: Yeah. *(to audience)* We might be able to let you out a little early tonight.

JESS: That'd be great.

ADAM: Because, see, we did all the Histories just now—

DANIEL: And we covered the Comedies in a lump—

JESS: Okay, that leaves the Tragedies. We did 'Titus Andronicus' with all the blood—

---

[82] *'Charles a turd'*; this section is not intended to cast aspersions on any particular member of Great Britain's Royal Family. Really, they're *all* a bunch of pasty-faced, inbred chowderheads, aren't they?

[83] *'Fergie'*; an odd reference, possibly to an obscure former member of the Royal Family, know nowadays mostly in fashion circles for popularizing the 'sunburnt nipple look,' or to former Chicago Cubs Hall-of-Famer Ferguson Jenkins, known nowadays mostly for his fastball. In either case, a very dated reference indeed.

ADAM: 'Romeo and Juliet' we did—

DANIEL: 'Julius Caesar,' 'Troilus and Cressida,' right—

JESS: We rapped 'Othello,' and Lear was in the football game, 'Macbeth' we did with Scottish accents. What about 'Antony and Cleopatra?'

ADAM: Yeah, I vomited on that lady over there—

JESS: Right. 'Timon of Athens' I mentioned. 'Coriolanus?'

ADAM: I don't want to do that one.

DANIEL: Why? What's the matter with 'Coriolanus?'

ADAM: I don't like the 'anus' part. I think it's offensive.

JESS: Okay, so we skip the anus play.[84]

DANIEL: And that's it, right? That's all of them.

JESS: Hey, you guys... *(Points to a spot in the program.)*

ALL: Oh, no. 'Hamlet!'

JESS: How could we forget 'Hamlet?'

---

[84] *'the anus play'*; since the RSC bypasses *Coriolanus* rather precipitously, we should note that this work is not entirely original to Shakespeare. It is in fact based on an heroic poem by the little-known Irish bard Seamus McFlynn. McFlynn's work was performed at the ceremonial opening of Trinity College, Dublin, in 1592, and deals with an arrogant Irish chieftain of the eighth century who defeats an army of pagans and leprechauns to bring Christianity to County Sligo. Shakespeare used this Irish tragedy of *Cory O'Lanus* as the basis for his play.

The Anus Play

DANIEL: I dunno. It's right there.

ADAM: Shakespeare didn't write 'Hamlet,' did he?[85]

JESS: Of course he did.

ADAM: I thought it was a Mel Gibson movie.

JESS: Ladies and gentlemen, thirty-six plays down, one to go. Perhaps the greatest play ever written in the English language. A play of such lofty poetic and philo—

ADAM *(tugging at* JESS' *sleeve)*: Wait a minute, Jess. 'Hamlet' is a really serious, hard-core play, and I'm just not up for it right now.

JESS: Whaddaya mean? It's the last one. We've done thirty-six already!

ADAM: I know. It's just that that football game left me emotionally and physically drained, and I just don't think that I could do justice to it.

JESS: We don't have to do justice to it. We just have to do it.

ADAM *(slinking into audience)*: I don't wanna do it!

---

[85] *'Shakespeare didn't write "Hamlet," did he?'*; of course, there is a pile of scholarly debate the size of Antarctica, and just about as interesting, about whether Shakespeare wrote anything at all, if he in fact existed. For the record, this editor firmly believes that Shakespeare existed, wrote most or all the plays he's supposed to have written, and was a sexual dynamo. Then again, this editor also firmly believes that Jesus Christ was actually a transvestite sack-cloth salesman from a small planet in the lesser spiral arm of the Andromeda Galaxy; so reader beware!

The Compleat Wks of Willm Shkspr (Abridged)

DANIEL: Look, Adam. Our show's called 'The Complete Works of William Shakespeare.' *(indicating audience)* I think they'd like to see 'Hamlet.'

ADAM: Okay, so we'll call it 'The Complete Works of William Shakespeare Except Hamlet.'

JESS *(following* ADAM *into audience)*: That's the most ridiculous thing I've ever heard!

ADAM: Well if YOU wanna do it, then do it. I don't have to if I don't want to. I'll just sit here with this guy/lady. *(Sits on an audience member's lap.)* He/she's my friend. I'll sit here and watch you two do it.

DANIEL: C'mon Adam—

   (JESS and DANIEL *try to pry him loose from the audience member, but* ADAM *starts to get hysterical.)*

ADAM: You can't make me do it! You can't!

JESS *(to audience member)*: Hey! Leggo of our actor!

ADAM: Okay, okay! Just don't touch me.

DANIEL: Are you alright?

ADAM: I'm fine.

JESS: We're going to do 'Hamlet' now, right?

ADAM: Yeah.

JESS: Okay. Geez, have a cow! *(tossing a now-crumpled wad back to the audience member)* Here's your program back. Sorry, it got kinda trashed. *(to* DANIEL*)* Right. We start off with the guard scene, so we need Bernardo and Horatio.

DANIEL: We'll need Rosencrantz and Guildenstern.

JESS: Nah, they've got their own play, we can skip them.

(While JESS *is distracted,* ADAM *sprints toward the exit at the back of the theater.)*

Hey, where do you think you're going?!

(JESS sprints after him. ADAM *sees he's being chased and grabs an audience member.)*

ADAM: I'll kill this guy/lady! I'll kill him/her![86]

JESS: You leave him/her alone!

(ADAM lets go of his victim and darts for the door.)*

JESS *(chasing him out of the theater)*: Get back here this instant, you Shakespeare wimp!!

(ADAM runs out the back of the house. JESS *follows, slamming the door behind him. We hear* ADAM *scream once in the lobby, and then silence. They are gone.* DANIEL *follows them a little way up the aisle, then stops. He returns to the stage alone.)*

---

[86] *'kill him/her'*; this form is of course used only if Adam has grabbed a hermaphrodite. Otherwise, he usually just says, 'it.' On a deeper level: killing of audience members is generally considered illegal and immoral, except during a performance of *Joseph and the Amazing Technicolor Dreamcoat*, when it is considered euthanasia. (See note on *'vomit,'* footnote 69)

DANIEL: Jess is usually much faster than Adam. I'm sure they'll be right back.

(DANIEL stalls.)[87]

Why don't we take the intermission here. Go out to the lobby, stretch your legs, get something to eat; we've got some Reduced Shakespeare Company t-shirts for sale if you'd like one of those. I'll meet you back here in fifteen minutes. Adam and Jess should be back by then, and we will proceed with 'Hamlet, Prince of Denmark'—I hope.

(DANIEL exits as a roller-skating prop girl scoops up assorted swords, wigs, and severed heads. Lights come up in the house. It's...)

---

[87] *'Daniel stalls'*; through the years, the actors who have played this role have been forced to plumb new depths in creating ways to stall after Jess' and Adam's disappearance. Daniel, for example, has an extremely likable onstage persona, a nice smile, sparkly eyes, and cute buns, so he just stood there. Daniel's replacement, Reed Martin, had no such luxury, and was forced to whistle the theme song to *Leave It To Beaver*, play *The William Tell Overture* on his throat, eat fire, roast a marshmallow, and, in perhaps the greatest debasement of the Shakespearean actor's art since Adam's work in the previous scene, play 'The Telephone Waltz' on the accordion. Of course, Reed's training as a Ringling Bros./Barnum & Bailey clown was indispensable in this scene, even though the audience's attention to the narrative thread of the show was often distracted by his stereotypical clown characteristics: big feet, orange hair, and a barely-concealed secret desire to kill all the bad little children and entomb them in a cocoon of cotton candy.

INTERMISSION[88]

The script's authors were unable to agree on the purpose and symbolism of the 'Intermission,' so they have each provided their own assessment. The editor expresses no preference, but submits to the tyranny of the philosophical implications of both Relativity theory, that each is probably 'true' in a subjective sense, and of Chaos theory, that as stupid as it sounds it all makes sense somehow.

Adam notes:

> Hamlet really is a hard-core play. It's got at least five acts, it's over four hours long, and it's filled with hard to pronounce names like 'Fortinbras' and 'Betelgeuse.'[89] So if your partners decide that they want to perform it, I suggest you get out of the theater as quickly as possible. If you are being pursued by one of your fellow actors you have three possible options:
>
> 1. Run very fast.
> 2. Pretend to be dead.
> 3. Actually be dead.
>
> There is a fourth option, which is to kill your fellow actors. But this is

---

[88] *'intermission'*; in Britain the 'intermission' is called the 'interval.' Furthermore, 'chips' are called 'crisps,' and 'fries' are called 'chips.' The second floor of a building is referred to as 'the first floor,' and tepid water pathetically dribbling into a tub is known throughout the U.K. as 'a shower.' Whereas in the United States the word 'shag' refers to a type of carpet, in the British Isles the term is a slang expression for 'Beaver Hunting with your One-Eyed Trouser Snake.'

[89] *'Betelgeuse'*; there is of course no character in *Hamlet* named 'Betelgeuse.' There used to be, but he vanished mysteriously.

generally considered illegal (except when performing *Joseph and the Amazing Technicolor Dreamcoat*—see footnotes).

Jess notes:

Intermission is definitely my favorite part of the show. While Adam is running around in a paranoid homicidal frenzy, I disguise myself as an audience member, slip down to the bar for a lovely, refreshing, alcoholic beverage, and stand around in the lobby chatting up potential groupies. 'These guys are hysterical, aren't they? I hear Jess is really great in the sack,' is a terrific conversation-starter.

Daniel notes:

Actually Jess and Adam run straight to the dressing room to talk about the audience for fifteen minutes. After a serious effort to adjust my dance belt so it isn't riding up quite so high, I join the debate about which audience member was enjoying the show the least, so that we could pick on him/her/it during Act Two.

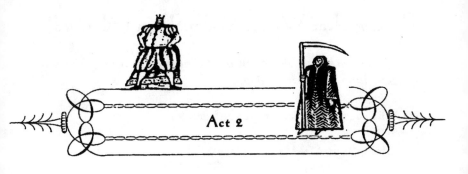

Act 2

(The intermission music fades out and lights come up—on an empty stage. After a beat, DANIEL *enters nervously, in costume for the opening of* Hamlet.*)*

DANIEL *(to audience)*: Hi. *(He waits for a response, then...)* Have a nice intermission? *(He again waits for a response.)* Yeah? What'd you do? *(He waits for a response.)* Was there a long line at the Ladies' room? *(Of course there was.)* Yeah, I hate that. Um, Jess and Adam aren't back yet. Actually, Jess called during the intermission. He found Adam at the airport, trying to catch a flight out of here. He said until they got back, I should cover the sonnets. *(pause)* Shakespeare wrote one hundred and fifty-four sonnets.[90] I've condensed them down onto this three-by-five card *(he produces one)*, and I was thinking maybe what we could do is pass it among the audience. Like if we start right here with you; *(indicating a member of the audience)* you take it, read it, enjoy it, then pass it to the person next to you and so on down the row, and then you pass it behind you, and so on, back and forth and back and forth and back and forth. And back and forth and back and forth and back, and by the time it gets to you *(in the back)* Jess and Adam should be here. So if we could have some house lights here...just take it, read it, pass it to the person next to you.

---

[90] *'one hundred and fifty-four sonnets'*; while this is a substantial number of sonnets, it should be remembered that Isaac Asimov has written over five hundred books (though his output was slowed somewhat by his death in 1992), so Shakespeare is no big deal.

(JESS enters at the back of the house, dragging the still-unwilling ADAM behind him.)

DANIEL: Jess and Adam, ladies and gentlemen!

(JESS drags ADAM to the stage.)

JESS: Sorry it took so long...

ADAM *(crying)*: I don't wanna do it. It's just so big. It's got so many words...

JESS: We can do it, man. We know 'Hamlet' backwards and forwards.[91]

(ADAM begins to hack and cough.)

Oh, not this again! *(Holds up his shirt for ADAM to honk his nose into.)* Here, Adam. Blow. Blow! *(He does.)* Daniel, take him backstage and get him together. I'll take the intro out here.

(DANIEL and ADAM exit. JESS looks at the snot in his shirt.)

JESS: I bet Laurence Olivier doesn't have to do this... Well, not anymore, anyway.[92] *(to light booth)* Bob, can I have a little bit

---

[91] *'backwards and forwards'*; an excellent example of the dramatic technique of 'foreshadowing,' where the playwright holds his foreskin up to a bright light source and makes a shadow on the wall that looks exactly like George Washington's head.

[92] *'Laurence Olivier...not anymore, anyway'*; this reference first appeared in the show the night the late Lord Olivier, perhaps the greatest Shakespearean actor of this century, shuffled off the mortal coil in July, 1989. The fact that the line remains intact as of this script's recording in July, 1992, must reflect one of two facts: 1) Olivier is so revered and/or despised in the collective unconscious that even after three years, his death still haunts the Shakespearean theater; or 2) Jess was simply too lazy to write another joke. Scholars unfamiliar with Jess' personal habits of dress, hygiene, and morality may incline toward the former; this editor emphatically believes the latter.

of mood lighting out here please, to set the scene for perhaps the greatest play ever written in the English language. 'Hamlet...the Tragedy...of the Prince...of Denmark.' The place: Denmark.[93] The time: a very long time ago. The battlements of Elsinore castle, round about midnight. Two guards enter. *(Exits. After a beat, we hear from offstage, sotto voce:)* Well, go on, Adam. Get out there.

ADAM *(o.s.)*: No. I don't wanna.

JESS *(o.s.)*: C'mon, you said you would.

ADAM *(o.s.)*: No, no, no...

(The escalating backstage argument is cut off by the abrupt sound of a slap, followed by the sound of ADAM *blowing his nose.* ADAM *enters as* BERNARDO, *wiping his nose;* DANIEL *enters opposite as* HORATIO.)*

A/BERNARDO: "Who's there?

D/HORATIO: Nay, answer me. Stand and unfold yourself.[94]

A/BERNARDO: Long live the King.

---

[93] *'the place—Denmark'*; that *Hamlet, Prince of Denmark* is set in Denmark has long been widely accepted. Professor Oeufpate, however, makes an intriguing case for relocating Elsinore to a swampy region of what is now known as Zimbabwe. This piece of shoddy scholarship would not be mentioned here except for the fact that this editor really likes writing the word 'Zimbabwe.' Zimbabwe, Zimbabwe, Zimbabwe.

[94] *'Stand and unfold yourself'*; in the garbled First Quarto edition of 1603, "Stand and unfold, unspindle, and unmutilate yourself!"

The Compleat Wks of Willm Shkspr (Abridged)

D/HORATIO: Bernardo?[95]

A/BERNARDO: He. 'Tis now struck twelve. Get thee to bed, Horatio.

D/HORATIO: For this relief, much thanks.

A/BERNARDO: Well, good night.

D/HORATIO: Peace, break thee off. Look where it comes!

(The ghost of Hamlet's father enters. Well, it's actually just a sweat sock with a happy face drawn on it in Marks-a-Lot, dangling from a fishing line upstage center. But it's ver-ry scar-ry nevertheless. JESS *makes ghostly moaning sounds from backstage.)*

A/BERNARDO: Mark it, Horatio. It would be spoke to.

D/HORATIO: What art thou? By heaven, I charge thee, speak!

*(*JESS *makes the sound of a cock crowing, and the sock*

---

[95] *'Bernardo'*; Adam has often wondered aloud, 'if this is Denmark, how come there's a character named Bernardo?' The answer, Adam, reflects on one of the more interesting quirks of historical cultural geography. During the 'English Renaissance' of Queen Elizabeth's reign (1558-1603), the Renaissance in Italy was nearly a century old. During the peak of Venetian power under the Doges, Venetian merchant marines had developed an enormous trade throughout Europe in what was, for the time, a revolutionary concept: pizza delivery. In fact, Venetian delivery boys of the Two Swarthy Guys from Italy Company often made deliveries to the nations of Scandinavia, although because it was far from downtown Venice and outside the 10-league 'free delivery' radius, the gondola driver would expect a very large tip indeed. Many of these pizza pioneers were amazed by the rugged beauty and subzero temperatures of the Great North and returned immediately to Venice. Many more were impressed with the fun-loving nature of the people who named their country after a breakfast pastry, and decided to stay. Hence, Luigis, Tonys, Marias, and, yes, Bernardos hailing from Copenhagen were quite common in Shakespeare's day.

disappears.)

'Tis gone.

A/BERNARDO: It was about to speak when the cock crew.[96]

D/HORATIO: Break we our watch up;[97] and by my advice, let us impart what we have seen tonight unto...

BOTH: Hamlet, Prince of Denmark!

(They exit together. JESS enters as HAMLET.[98] He is classically costumed: black tights, pants, doublet, hat and dagger.)

HAM: O that this too too solid flesh would melt,
Thaw,[99] and resolve itself into a dew.
That it should come to this, but two months dead.
So loving to my mother. Frailty, thy name is woman.
(pointing to a woman in the audience) —Yeah, you!
Married with mine uncle, my father's brother

---

[96] *'the cock crew'*; throughout its 12-year existence, the RSC has refrained from making any joke regarding male genitalia with this line. However, by this point in the show the audience has become so accustomed to the RSC's sophisticated sense of humor that they generally *assume* there was one, and laugh anyway.

[97] *'break we our watch up'*; successfully kept out of the show while Daniel was in the Company, Adam and Reed overrode Jess' objections to include a bit where Bernardo and Horatio gleefully smash invisible wristwatches with their swords. This bit of physical business currently ranks second only to *'bone appètit'* (q.v. footnote 50) as the worst joke in the show.

[98] *'Hamlet'*; recent culino-linguistic research indicates that Shakespeare intended Young Hamlet as a metaphor for pork or ham, while Claudius is symbolic of beef by-products. Of course, this makes Ophelia a starter salad, and the whole play can be seen as an allegory of a high-cholesterol diet.

[99] *'flesh would...thaw'*; Hamlet is obviously defrosting some pork chops.

Thy funeral baked meats[180] did coldly furnish forth
The marriage tables.

(He kneels and begins sobbing uncontrollably; a very impressive display of melancholy, a performance that William Shatner himself would be proud of. HORATIO and BERNARDO appear in the up left doorway, and watch Hamlet bawl. BERNARDO nods for Horatio to approach him. HORATIO enters as BERNARDO disappears.)

D/HORATIO: My lord!

J/HAMLET: Horatio!

(They exchange a very silly Wittenberg University Danish Club handshake.)

Methinks I see my father.

D/HORATIO: Where, my lord?

J/HAMLET: In my mind's eye, Horatio.

D/HORATIO: My lord, I think I saw him yesternight.

J/HAMLET: Saw who?

D/HORATIO: The king, your father.

J/HAMLET: The king my father? But where was this?

---

[180] *'funeral baked meats'*; note again Hamlet's obsession with meat. The frequency of references to meat, and especially to pork, in *Hamlet* lends considerable credence to the theory that Shakespeare's plays were in fact written by Francis Bacon.

D/HORATIO: Upon the platform where we watched.

J/HAMLET: 'Tis very strange. I will watch tonight.
Perchance 'twill[181] walk again. All is not well.
Would the night were come.

(The stage lighting changes suddenly from a warm day wash to a cold midnight blue dappled with moonlight. The quick change catches JESS *and* DANIEL *off guard. They give a thumbs-up to the light booth, and commence acting cold.)*

J/HAMLET: The air bites shrewdly. It is very cold.

D/HORATIO: Look, my lord, it comes!

J/HAMLET: Angels and ministers of grace defend us.
Something is rotten in the state of Denmark.

(ADAM enters as the GHOST OF HAMLET'S FATHER.[182] *He wears a ghostly robe that is somewhat reminiscent of a sweat sock.)*

A/GHOST: Mark me![183]

---

[181] *'perchance 'twill'*; one of many embedded stage directions in Shakespeare's work, alerting us to the fabric the ghost wears. No detail, even of costume, is beneath Shakespeare's attention.

[182] *'the Ghost of Hamlet's Father'*; Adam offers this performance note regarding the Ghost: 'The character of the Ghost of Hamlet's Father should be based on Bela Lugosi. If you plan on researching this, I DO NOT suggest that you watch *Plan Nine from Outer Space.* Not only does Mr. Lugosi remain silent in *Plan Nine,* but he died halfway through the filming of the picture and was replaced by the director's wife's chiropractor.'

[183] *'Mark me'*; if we are to accept 'mark' as Elizabethan slang for 'homosexual' (see footnote 35) and further accept the legend that Shakespeare played the role of the Ghost in the original production of *Hamlet,* the phrase, 'mark me!' takes on interesting connotations as regards Shakespeare's sexual preference. And determining the sexual preference of famous dead playwrights, while politically incorrect and academically irrelevant, is big fun.

The Compleat Wks of Willm Shkspr (Abridged)

Shakespeare and his "Friends"
See footnotes 27, 183, et al., regarding Shakespeare's sexual preference.

J/HAMLET: Speak. I am bound to hear.

A/GHOST: So art thou to revenge when thou shalt hear.
  If ever thou didst thy dear father love
  Revenge his foul[184] and most unnatural murther.

J/HAMLET: Murther!

D/HORATIO: Murther![185]

A/GHOST: The serpent that did sting thy father's life
  Now wears his crown.

J/HAMLET: My uncle.

D/HORATIO: Your uncle!

A/GHOST: Let not the royal bed of Denmark
  Become a couch for incest.

J/HAMLET: Incest!

D/HORATIO: A couch!

A/GHOST: Adieu, Hamlet, remember me! *(Exits.)*

---

[184] *'revenge his foul'*; in the garbled First Quarto edition of 1603, 'revenge his fowl.' This supports the culinary interpretation of *Hamlet*, firmly placing Hamlet's father in the realm of poultry.

[185] *'murther'*; the Elizabethan spelling of 'murder.' One of the few instances where the RSC uses the archaic, rather than the modernized, spelling. Debate rages over the modernization of Shakespeare's spellings. A.A. Greg argues, 'To print banquet for banket, fathom for fadom, lantern for lanthorn, murder for murther, mushroom for mushrump, orphan for orphant, perfect for parfit, portcullis for perculace, wreck for wrack, and so on, and so on, is sheer perversion.' Greg is considered by most scholars to be a majer dikhed.

The Compleat Wks of Willm Shkspr (Abridged)

Daniel Singer as Polonius
Daniel, in typically pragmatic fashion, plays Polonius with subtlety and wit
while Jess and Adam verbally abuse and vomit on the audience in an
embarrassing competition for attention.

D/HORATIO: There are more things in heaven and earth, Horatio, Than are dreamt of in your philosophy. So... *(slapping him)* piss off.

(HORATIO exits.)

J/HAMLET: I hereafter shall think meet[186] to put an antic disposition on. The time is out of joint. O cursed spite that ever I was born to exit right.

(HAMLET tries to 'exit right' but smashes into the proscenium arch, falls down, gets up. He exits, we hear a crash in the wings, a roller skate rolls onstage and out the upstage left door.)

(DANIEL enters as POLONIUS. He watches the roller skate go offstage. He is a doddering old man. He takes his time, totters slowly downstage centers, adjusts his dentures, clears his throat, and...)

D/POLONIUS: Neither a borrower nor a lender be.

(He is tremendously satisfied with himself. He turns and waddles toward the upstage right door, where he is run over by ADAM, entering screaming as OPHELIA.)

A/OPHELIA: My lord, as I was sewing in my closet,
Lord Hamlet, with his doublet all unbraced,
No hat upon his head, pale as his shirt,
His knees knocking each other, and with a look
So piteous in purport as if he had been loosed

---

[186] *'I hereafter shall think meet'*; in the First Quarto, 'I hereafter shall think about meat.'

Ophelia: the Dream and the Reality
In this series of four classic renderings of Ophelia, the limitations of the
painter's art become painfully clear. Even these great masterpieces cannot
capture the wistful beauty of Adam's portrayal.

Out of hell to speak of horrors, he comes before me.[187]

D/POLONIUS: Mad for thy love?

A/OPHELIA: I know not.

D/POLONIUS: Why, this is the very ecstasy of love.
I have found the cause of Hamlet's lunacy.
Since brevity is the soul of wit,[188] I will be brief:
He is mad.

(HAMLET *enters reading a book, feigning madness.*)

Look you where the poor wretch comes reading.
Away, I do beseech you.

(OPHELIA *exits.*)

How does my good lord Hamlet?

J/HAMLET: Well, God-a-mercy.

---

[187] *'comes before me'*; scholarly debate over the author's intent in this line is extensive. Does Hamlet 'come before' Ophelia in space, or in time? That is, does he enter the room half undressed, and, grimacing 'as if he had been loosed out of hell,' bring himself to orgasm in front of her? Or do they engage in sexual congress, during which Hamlet experiences premature ejaculation, leaving Ophelia unsatisfied? Female scholars by and large argue the latter, while male scholars tend toward the former, interpretation. A synthesis of sorts was achieved in the recent XXX film adaptation of *Hamlet*, entitled *OFeelYa Up!* wherein both interpretations were explored simultaneously by two Hamlets and three Ophelias while Laertes and Gertrude watched. Adam disagrees with all these interpretations, and notes, 'obviously, Hamlet and Ophelia have been shagging in the closet.' Why he thinks the scene has anything to do with carpeting is entirely beyond this editor.
[188] *'brevity is the soul of wit'*; how true.

The Compleat Wks of Willm Shkspr (Abridged)

D/POLONIUS: Do you know me my lord?

J/HAMLET: Excellent well. You are a fishmonger.[189]

D/POLONIUS: What do you read, my lord?

J/HAMLET: Words, words, words.[190]

D/POLONIUS *(aside)*: Though this be madness, yet there's method in't."[191]

A/OPHELIA *(poking her head out from backstage)*: Daddy, the
    Players are here and they want to talk to you right away so
    you'd better get back here as soon as you can cuz they want
    something I dunno what they want but you'd better hurry.... *(She
    disappears. POLONIUS follows her off.)*

J/HAMLET: "I am but mad north-northwest. When the wind is
      southerly,
    I know a hawk from a handsaw.
    I'll have these players play something like
    The murder of my father before mine uncle.

---

[189] *'fishmonger'*; a bastardization of the Middle Franglais word, *fish-manger*, one who eats fish. This unquestionably puts Polonius' family in the symbolic realm of sea-food, and hence establishes the Polonius family as the diametrical opposite of Hamlet's red-meat orientation.

[190] *'Words, words, words'*; scholars now generally agree that this is not Hamlet's line of dialogue but, rather, Shakespeare's scribbled reminder to himself to come up with something appropriate here before opening night. Presumably it is an oversight that he, alas, never did.

[191] *'Though this be madness, yet there's method in't'*; the inspiration, as well as the justification, for Constantin Stanislavski's famous acting theory. It was the great Russian director's belief that he could train madmen from a local sanitarium to follow his acting directions perfectly and thereby gain a far 'truer' representation of his *auteur*'s vision than he could ever coax from rational actors; he could also save himself a few rubles in the process since the madmen were generally willing to work for crusts of bread and rat meat.

I'll observe his looks. If he do but blench,
I know my course. The play's the thing
Wherein I'll catch the conscience of the king!

(HAMLET *kneels and draws his dagger; with increasing intensity:*)

To be, or not to be? That is the question.[192]
Whether 'tis nobler in the mind to suffer
The slings and arrows of outrageous fortune
Or to take arms against a sea of troubles
And by opposing end them.
(He's really intense now; maybe a little too intense.)
                                        To die; to sleep;"
Or just to take a nap and hope you wake up
In time for dinner because you gotta make
guacamole for twelve[193] and you just can't take the pressure of
this speech!!![194]

---

[192]*'To be or not to be. That is the question'*; Ha! Made you look! You really
think we're stupid enough to even *try* to say something witty, profound, or
original about this line? Get a life, get a clue, and/or get stuffed!
[193]*'Guacamole for twelve'*;
Ingredients:

> 10 Ripe Avocados
> 1 Bottle Picante Salsa
> 1 Lemon, juiced
> 1/2 Cup diced onion
> 1 Clove garlic

Instructions: Mush ingredients together in a large bowl. Serve with tortilla chips.
Best when hunkered down in front of the tube for some Championship Wrestling
or Ice Hockey.
[194]*'this speech'*; Jess' unique interpretation of Hamlet's famous soliloquy has
been called, alternatively, 'A brilliant note of modern angst' (*Montreal Gazette*)
and 'A piece of crap' (Jess' mother). This editor, always suspicious of the press,
is inclined to agree with Jess' mother.

The Compleat Wks of Willm Shkspr (Abridged)

(JESS collapses into a heap. DANIEL *and* ADAM *rush in to comfort him.)*

I can't do it!

ADAM: Jess, look, Daniel and I have been talking about it backstage, and you don't have to go on with the speech if you don't want to.

JESS: I'm so embarrassed.

ADAM: Ladies and gentlemen, you'll have to excuse him. It's a very heavy emotional speech, and he's been under a lot of pressure lately,[195] what with what happened with Felicia—

JESS: Felicia!!!!

DANIEL: Felicia is Jess' favorite character on General Hospital. He's upset because... *(DANIEL updates the audience on Felicia's trauma of the day.)*

ADAM: Yeah, so I think for tonight we should just skip this speech. I'm sorry if anybody feels ripped off, but we think it's a really overrated speech anyway. I mean, Hamlet is supposed to be thinking about killing his uncle and instead he's talking about killing himself, so we feel it just weakens the character. So we'll just skip it and move on to a later point in the play—

DANIEL: Shall we skip to the play-within-a-play sequence?

ADAM: Yeah. We'll just skip ahead, so you really don't miss anything—

---

[195] *'he's been under a lot of pressure lately'*; actually, he's been an emotional wreck as long as anyone can remember.

DANIEL: Wait a minute, there's that one other speech of Hamlet's. I don't know if we should cut it.

ADAM: Oh, the "What a piece of work is man" speech?

DANIEL: Yeah.

ADAM: Right. Well, there's this one speech that goes:
"I have of late, but wherefore I know not, lost all my mirth, forgone all custom of exercise; and indeed it goes so heavy with my disposition that this goodly frame, the earth, seems to me a sterile promontory; this most excellent canopy, the air, look you; this brave o'erhanging firmament, this majestic roof fretted with golden fire, why it appears to me no more than a foul and pestilent congregation of vapours. What a piece of work is man; how noble in reason, how infinite in faculty, in form and moving how express and admirable; in action how like an angel; in apprehension how like a god. The beauty of the world, the paragon of animals; and yet to me, what is this quintessence of dust? Man delights not me."[196]

(He has delivered the speech simply, quietly and without a trace of interpretation. You can hear a pin drop.)

DANIEL: So we'll skip that speech and go right to the killing.

(They all start to exit, then DANIEL *remembers:)*

Wait a minute. What about the "get thee to a nunnery" scene?

JESS: Oh yeah, let's do that one real quick...

---

[196] *'I have of late...man delights not me'*; Adam's interpretation of Hamlet's famous 'What a piece of work is man' soliloquy has been called 'poetically powerful' (*The Independent*) and 'A piece of crap' (Jess).

The Compleat Wks of Willm Shkspr (Abridged)

ADAM: No, we can't. I'm not in the right costume.

DANIEL: We have to. It's central to the plot.

ADAM: I can't! I'm not in the right character either. Ophelia is a very difficult and complex character.

DANIEL: No, it's easy.

ADAM: It's not.

DANIEL: It is. Anybody could play that character. My mother could play that character. That lady right there *(pointing to a woman in the audience)* could play that character.

JESS: Well let's get her to do it then. This is giving me a headache...

(JESS and DANIEL go and grab the 'Volunteer' from the audience, and bring her onstage.)

ADAM: You guys, this isn't fair. C'mon, Jess, I didn't make you do your speech. You can't just bring some bozo[197] onstage to play Ophelia!

JESS: She's not a bozo, and besides, she volunteered. *(to Volunteer)* Okay, first of all, what's your name?

---

[197] *'some bozo'*; a uniquely American reference to Bozo the Clown, a kiddie-show television host who shares the stereotypical attributes of all clowns (see footnote 87, regarding Reed Martin). Bozo burst back into the international limelight during the 1992 U.S. Presidential elections, when Democratic candidates Bill Clinton and Al Gore were referred to as 'bozos' by then-President George Bush, who also shares the stereotypical attributes of all clowns.

(She responds.)

Do you mind if we call you 'Bob?' It's a little easier to remember. Okay, Bob, this is a very simple scene—

ADAM: It's extremely difficult.

JESS: Hamlet has had this relationship with Ophelia, but what with what's been happening with his father and his mother and his uncle and yatta-yatta-yatta, he can't deal with her anymore—

ADAM: He's being a prick.

JESS: So he gets all worked up and tells her to get out of his life. He says, "Get thee to a nunnery." Now in our version of this scene, all that Ophelia does in response is, she screams. That's all she does. Hamlet says, "Get thee to a nunnery," and Ophelia screams. Okay? Let's give it a try.

ADAM *(shoving her slightly as he crosses past her)*: Good luck.

(A pause while JESS prepares by taking a few breaths and running his fingers through his hair.)

JESS: "Get thee to a nunnery!"

(The Volunteer screams—probably not very well.)

DANIEL: Did you hear that, Adam? I thought it was really good.

JESS: It was okay.

ADAM: No, it sucked, really. I mean, I don't mean to be catty, but you're not an actress, and frankly, it shows. You obviously had no idea what was going on inside Ophelia's head.

The Compleat Wks of Willm Shkspr (Abridged)

JESS: Actors use what they call 'subtext,' Bob.

DANIEL: Or 'inner monologue.'

ADAM: Exactly. That's what you didn't have, and as a result your performance was just flat and one-dimensional. But I think you showed a lot of heart! A lot of courage! A lot of—as Shakespeare would say—'chutzpah,' and I think we should WORKSHOP this. I think we could really make this a happening moment. In fact, *(to the light booth)* Bob? Could you bring up the house lights, please?

(The house lights come up.)

(to audience) Cuz I think we should get everybody involved in this.[198] You know, sort of create a supportive environment for Bob here *(indicating the Volunteer)*. Maybe we could get everybody to act out what's going on inside of Ophelia's head. Like, divide everybody up into Ophelia's Id, Ego, and Superego—[199]

JESS: Oh yeah, like a Freudian analysis!

---

[198] *'get everybody involved in this'*; Adam offers this performance note regarding the ensuing 'audience participation' section: 'Sometimes an audience is reluctant to participate to their fullest potential. We have found that this can be countered by bringing random audience members onstage at swordpoint and holding them hostage throughout the participation section. The resulting terror is extremely effective in guaranteeing that the onlookers will respond with gusto and verve when you, the performer, call upon them to do so. Especially if bloodshed is threatened. Furthermore, if there are any former members of the Reagan Administration in the theater, the hostages can be traded for TOW missiles at the end of the performance.
[199] *'Id, Ego, and Superego'*; in Jungian psychoanalysis, these facets of the mind are of course replaced by the archetypes Curly, Larry, and Moe, respectively.

ADAM: Yeah, a Floydian analysis![1180]

DANIEL: I get the Id!

JESS: Cool! I'll get the Ego.

(JESS grabs a guy out of the audience and hustles him up onstage.)

ADAM *(to the guy)*: Now you're playing the part of Ophelia's ego. At this point in the play her ego is flighty, it's confused... it's an Ego on the run.

JESS: Oh, great! So we'd like you to symbolize this, Bob, by—oh, do you mind if we call you 'Bob?'—we'll symbolize this by actually having you run back and forth across the stage in front of Ophelia. Will you give that a try? Right now, just...

ALL: Go, go, go, go, go, go!

(Ego runs.)

DANIEL: Okay, now everyone in the front three rows, you're going to be Ophelia's Id. Now her Id is confused, it's wishy-washy, it's awash in a sea of alternatives. So everybody, hands in the air, wave them back and forth, kind of undulate, and say, *(in falsetto)* 'Maybe... maybe not... maybe... maybe not.' Okay, that's good. Save some for later.

JESS *(picking on a less-than-enthusiastic member of the Id)*: Right. What was your problem? YOU were not participating with the rest of the group. You know what that means, don't you? You're going to have to do it—

[1180] *'Floydian analysis'*; Adam has obviously confused Sigmund Freud, the father of modern psychology, with the groundbreaking English rock group, Pink Floyd. 'Yeah, I love that record, *Dark Side of the Subconscious,'* Adam notes.

The Compleat Wks of Willm Shkspr (Abridged)

ALL: ALL...BY...YOUR...SELF.

DANIEL: Now, don't be embarrassed, nobody's watching.

(They make the malingerer do it alone.)

ADAM: I dunno, I feel a lot of love in this room. Now why don't we get everybody behind the front three rows to be Ophelia's Superego. This is the final psychological component. The Superego is those strong, moralistic voices inside your head that tell you exactly what to do. They're very powerful, very difficult to shake...some people never shake them in their whole lifetime...sorta like Catholicism.[1181] It's a very complex part of the psyche, so—Jess, why dontcha help me out on this.

JESS *(drawing out his sword)*: Okay.

ADAM: Why don't we divide the Superego into three parts? Let's have everybody from where Jess is indicating...

[1181] *'Catholicism'*; this editor must lay scholarly reserve aside for a moment and tell a joke. Stop me if you've heard it. A guy, we'll call him Fred, dies and goes to Hell, and he discovers it's not so bad. He wakes up in a clean, simple hotel room with cable television and decent room service. He orders up a Bloody Mary and gazes out the window; there's an adequate 9-hole golf-course outside, a small pool, jacuzzi, and a rather nice private lagoon with clear water and good reefs for snorkeling. He goes outside and there's Mephistopheles waiting in a golf cart, ready to give him a tour. Mephisto shows Fred the gym, the tennis courts, the family-style Italian restaurant. 'This is a pretty nice place,' Fred comments. 'Well, we like it,' Mephistopheles responds. 'Of course, the restaurants are nicer in Heaven, and they have an 18-hole golf course.' Just then, the cart zips over a rise, and in the distance, Fred sees a horrible fiery pit, spewing sulfurous ash into an Apocalypse sky; naked souls scream and wail as they plummet into the ever-consuming flames. 'Yow! What's that?', Fred wonders. 'Oh, don't worry about that,' Mephistopheles says as he bangs a U-turn and heads back to the hotel, 'we built that for the Catholics. They *insisted* on it!'

(JESS, indicating with his dagger, slices off the left third of the audience.)

...to my left be Section 'A.' Everyone from Jess to here *(indicating the middle third of the audience)*, you're Section 'B.' And everyone from here over to my right, you're section...? *(He seems to be prompting the audience to respond. They call out, 'C')* Yeah, it's not too bloody difficult, is it? Now section A is the masculine part of Ophelia's brain, the animus, so to speak. And I'd like you to use Hamlet's line for this. I'd like you to say, "Get thee to a nunnery!" Let's try it. Section A?

(They respond.)

DANIEL: Section A, that was awful.

ADAM: C'mon, people, work with me on this. We want it very loud, very strident. Section A?

(They respond.)

JESS: Yes! Much less totally pathetic!

ADAM: Okay, Section B. You're the voice of vanity, saying, for God's sake, do something with yourself. Put on some makeup or something—*(to the Volunteer)* no offense—really, this is straight out of the Shakespearean text. *(back to the audience)* I'd like you all to say, "Paint an inch thick!" Section B?

(They respond.)

Oooh. Section A could learn something from Section B. Okay, now Section C, we've saved you for last because you're the most important component of them all, because we're going to use you to draw this into a modern context, because we want

Ophelia to be relevant to women of today. So maybe she wants power...but she doesn't want to lose her femininity. She wants to be a corporate executive, but she wants to have babies at the same time. And somewhere deep in her psyche she's tired of being the waifish hippie chick, and she wants to assert herself *(He's starting to get carried away.)* and she just feels like saying, 'Look, cut the crap, Hamlet, my biological clock is ticking and I want babies now!' It's that angst-ridden—

JESS *(to the audience)*: So why don't we have you say that?

ADAM: Okay, yeah, Section C, we'll have you say...

ALL: 'Cut the crap, Hamlet, my biological clock is ticking, and I want babies now!'

ADAM: Let's give it a try, shall we? Section C?

(They respond. To the Volunteer.)

So now, Bob. We're going to get all of these elements in play, the Id, the Ego, the Superego—

JESS: The biological clock—

DANIEL: Maybe, maybe not—

ADAM: Now your job as an actress is to take all of these elements, synthesize them within your soul, then, at that moment of truth, we're going to build everyone into a mighty frenzy, stop everything, all attention goes to you, and you let out with that scream that epitomizes Ophelia. Ah, she can't wait. And remember, no matter what happens...

ALL: Act natural.

ADAM: Okay, start with the Ego.

JESS: Ready, Bob, on your mark, get set, go!

(The 'Ego' runs back and forth across the stage.)

DANIEL: Id, arms up. 'Maybe, maybe not...'

ADAM *(building to mighty frenzy)*: Section A... Section B... Section C... A... B... C... C... A, B, A, C, BABCA. Okay, STOP!

(ALL INDICATE THAT OPHELIA SHOULD SCREAM. As she does, she is hit with a red spotlight. Her scream ends, the audience goes wild, she bows. ADAM is kissing her feet. DANIEL removes ADAM'S tongue from her shoes and escorts her back to her seat. The house lights fade out as JESS and ADAM exit.)

DANIEL: Boy, we really shared something there, didn't we? But we digress.[1182] Back to 'Hamlet,' Act Three, Scene Two, the famous 'play-within-a-play scene,' in which Hamlet discovers conclusive evidence that his uncle murdered his father.

(HAMLET enters, pauses, then whips his hands out from behind his back to reveal sock-puppet Players on his hands.)

J/HAMLET: "Speak the speech, I pray you, as I pronounced it to you, trippingly on the tongue.[1183] Suit the action to the word, the

---

[1182] *'we digress'*; no kidding.

[1183] *'trippingly on the tongue'*; Shakespeare scholars at the University of California at Berkeley maintain that this refers to the earliest recorded experimentation with LSD-laced paper, or 'blotter acid.' Was Shakespeare, in fact, high as a kite when he wrote his greatest tragedies? Is Othello really the name of a highly potent variety of *Cannabis Indica*? Did the Moor strangle Desdemona because he was incredibly strung out? It's all interesting *(cont.)*

word to the action, and hold, as 'twere, the mirror up to nature.

(POLONIUS *enters, carrying a puppet theater which he sets center stage. The marquee reads, 'Ye Royal Theatre of Denmark')*

Will my lord hear this piece of work?[1184]

D/POLONIUS: Aye, and the king, too, presently.

(ADAM *enters as* CLAUDIUS. *He is not a nice man.*)

A/CLAUDIUS: And now, how does my cousin Hamlet, and my son?

J/HAMLET: A little more than kin, and less than kind.[1185]

A/CLAUDIUS: I have nothing with this answer Hamlet, these words are not mine."

D/POLONIUS: Take a seat, my lord.

(CLAUDIUS *takes a seat in the audience, moving a paying patron from his seat.*)

---

speculation, to be sure, but, for this editor, still overly hypothetical. The only evidence that will convince him, in fact, would be a tab of the stuff, sent in a plain brown envelope c/o Applause Books.

[1184] *'piece of work'*; in the Second Quarto of 1604, 'piece of crappe.'

[1185] *'and less than kind'*; the Second Quarto has the variation 'and less than kine'. *Kine* is an archaic plural for 'cow'. A typographical error, perhaps, but 'kine' does rhyme better with the next line's 'mine'. If correct, this line would seem to have Hamlet answering his uncle, 'A little more than your nephew, and less than cows,' an exceptionally odd reading unless the meat interpretation of the entire play is given credence.

The Royal Theater of Denmark is proud to present 'The Murther of Gonzago.'[1186] My lord, Act One.

(The puppet players enact a romantic dumbshow, the King puppet and Queen puppet meeting, falling in love, and promptly humping...POLONIUS breaks in.)

Intermission!

J/HAMLET: "How likes my lord the play?

A/CLAUDIUS: The lady doth protest too much, methinks!" *(to a man in the audience)* Get it? Get it? *(to the rest of the audience)* He doesn't get it.

D/POLONIUS: My lord, Act Two.

A/CLAUDIUS: Gesundheit.[1187]

(Act Two begins. The puppet King yawns, stretches, and lies down to sleep. A puppet shark dressed like Claudius appears and begins to eat the King! CLAUDIUS rises, storms onstage, rips the puppets off of HAMLET'S hands.)

[1186] *'Gonzago'*; Adam wonders, 'if this is Denmark, how come there's a character named 'Gonzago?'

Jess responds, 'Adam fails to note that, aside from apocryphal tales of Venetian Renaissance pizza-delivery boys delivering their pepperonis to Danish maidens in the early quattrocentro (see footnote 95), Hamlet himself says that the story of the murder of Gonzago "is extant, and written in very choice Italian." (III.ii.58-59). This accounts for the Italian bias, at least in the play-within-a-play. Gonzago is also rumored to have been the name of the brother of 'Bernardo' and the illicit lover of 'Reynaldo' who appears in Act V.'

Adam notes, 'Yeah, maybe. But these guys still sound more like the cast of the Sharks in West Side Story than members of the court in Denmark.'

To which Jess replies in flawless Latin, *'Adamus cuniculus inscius est.'* (literally, 'Adam is one dumb bunny.)

[1187] *'Act II—Gesundheit'*; until the advent of post-structuralist dramatic criticism, widely acknowledged to be the worst joke in the entire show.

The Compleat Wks of Willm Shkspr (Abridged)

D/POLONIUS: The king rises.

A/CLAUDIUS: "Give o'er the play! Lights! Away! *(Exits, taking the puppet theater.)*

J/HAMLET: I'll take the ghost's word for a thousand pound!

D/POLONIUS: My lord, the queen would speak with you in her closet.[1188]

J/HAMLET: Then will I come to my mother. *(Exits.)*

D/POLONIUS: Behind the arras I'll convey myself to hear the process. *(He hides in the doorway upstage left.)*

(Enter HAMLET and ADAM as GERTRUDE, opposite.)

J/HAMLET: Now, mother, what's the matter?

A/GERTRUDE: Hamlet, thou hast thy father much offended.[1189]

J/HAMLET *(drawing his dagger)*: Mother, you have my father much offended.[1190]

[1188] *'in her closet'*; Professor Oeufpate, in his wide-ranging work, *Great Unanswered Questions of Theater*, wonders, 'What the hell is she doing in the closet?' Adam is compelled to note, 'Presumably, this is the same closet where Hamlet and Ophelia were shagging earlier.'

[1189] *'offended'*; by shagging in his father's closet. On top of his good suit no less. Adam's 'closet' interpretation begins slowly to infect these heretofore academically sound glosses, and to supplant the editor's carefully constructed 'meat' interpretation.

[1190] *'offended'*; apparently, Gertrude has been shagging in the closet, too. It must be a very BIG closet.

A/GERTRUDE: What wilt thou do? Thou wilt not murder me? Help! Help! [1191] *(Exits.)*

D/POLONIUS: Help! Help!

J/HAMLET *(hearing Polonius)*: How now? A rat!

(HAMLET charges at POLONIUS with his dagger. He is just about to strike, when he suddenly shifts into SLOW MOTION. We hear Psycho-style horror music and the lights strobe as the dagger plunges into POLONIUS' armpit. POLONIUS exits as he dies. HAMLET licks his dagger clean and snaps out of slo-mo.)

J/HAMLET: Dead for a ducat, dead![1192]

(CLAUDIUS enters.)

A/CLAUDIUS: Now, Hamlet, where's Polonius?

J/HAMLET: At supper.

A/CLAUDIUS: At supper? Where?

J/HAMLET: Not where he eats, but where he is eaten."

(DANIEL enters as LAERTES. He's young, dashing, all fired up and rarin' to go.)

A/CLAUDIUS AND J/HAMLET: O no, it's Laertes!

[1191]Post-Freudian scholars have often cited the closet scene as evidence that Hamlet has an Oedipus Complex (i.e., he is secretly sexually attracted to his mother, wants to kill his father, and finds Sophocles' *Oedipus Rex* too Complex to read in Ancient Greek).

[1192]*'Dead for a ducat, dead!'*; so reads the First Folio. Second Quarto reads, 'Dead! For a ducat, dead!', while the First Quarto reads, 'Shit! Killed the wrong dude!'

A/CLAUDIUS: Son of Polonius.

J/HAMLET: Brother to Ophelia!

A/CLAUDIUS: And a snappy dresser![1193]

D/LAERTES: Why, thanks.
"O, thou vile king! Give me my father!
I'll be revenged for Polonius' murder.

(JESS *screams offstage, imitating Ophelia.* CLAUDIUS *exits.*)

How now, what noise is this?

(JESS *screams again.*)

Dear maid, kind sister, sweet Ophelia!

(OPHELIA *enters screaming, with flowers.*)

A/OPHELIA: They bore him barefaced on the bier
With a hey-nonny-nonny, hey-nonny
And in his grave rained many a tear
With a hey-nonny-nonny ha-cha-cha.[1194]

[1193] '*a snappy dresser*'; a prime example of the RSC's penchant for inserting updated political, topical and local references while on the road. 'A snappy dresser' is the failsafe default line. Usually, the RSC would substitute the name of a notorious bad guy, such as 'an Exxon executive,' 'the author of *The Satanic Verses*,' 'a Pistons fan,' 'a Republican,' 'a Canada Bell employee,' etc. (These jokes positively define the phrase 'you had to be there.') Just for fun, Laertes has also been 'no Jack Kennedy' and 'a known transvestite' among other things lost to posterity.

[1194] '*hey-nonny-nonny ha-cha-cha*'; Ophelia's 'mad song' is sung to the tune of the English traditional round, 'Country Life' In fact, all songs in the RSC production are sung either to this tune or to 'Greensleeves.' Not only does the constant use of the two tunes reinforce the themes of loss and hope which *(cont.)*

Fare you well my dove."
I'm mad! *(She is tossing flowers wildly about.)* I'm out of my
tiny little mind! *(to the Volunteer who played Ophelia)* See, this
is acting. Here's rue for you, and rosemary for remembrance...
and I would have given you violets, but they withered all when
my father died." I'm starting to feel a little nauseous...[1195]

(ADAM falls into the audience and pretends to vomit on people.)

I'm sorry. I'm so sick 'cause I'm about to die. Brrrappp!

D/LAERTES *(attempting to carry on despite the chaos* ADAM *is
creating in the audience)*: "Hamlet comes back—"

ADAM *(leaping back to the stage)*: Daniel, what's the next scene
with Ophelia?

DANIEL: What?

ADAM: What's the next scene with Ophelia?

DANIEL: There are no more scenes with Ophelia.

ADAM: No, c'mon. I'm up for it.

DANIEL: That's all Shakespeare wrote.

ADAM: Well, what happens to her?

---

are central to the message of the play, but they are the only Elizabethan tunes the
troupe knows. After a brief experiment in setting Ophelia's 'mad song' to the
tune of Yes' 1973 art-rock epic 'The Revealing Science of God,' the authors
decided to stick with the peppier 'Country Life'
[1195] *'a little nauseous'*; Adam's urge to vomit incessantly throughout the show is
one which has been shared by many critics.

Ophelia about to blow chunks

DANIEL: She drowns.

ADAM: Oh. Okay. *(Exits.)*

D/LAERTES: "Hamlet comes back: what would I undertake
To show myself my father's son in deed
More than in words? To—"

(OPHELIA re-enters with a cup of water.)

A/OPHELIA: Here I go. *(She throws the cup of water in her own face.)* Aaaaaaaaauugh! *(Dies, bows, exits.)*

D/LAERTES: "...To cut his throat in the church.
Aye, and to that end, I'll anoint my sword
With an unction so mortal that where it draws blood
No cataplasm[1196] can save the thing from this compulsion."
Huh?

(LAERTES exits. HAMLET enters, singing a tune. This time he whips out from behind his back...a skull.)

J/HAMLET: "This skull had a tongue in it, and could sing once.
Alas, poor Yorick! I knew him—
But soft! Here comes the queen.
(He goes to hide in the audience.)
Couch me awhile, and mark.[1197]

[1196] *'cataplasm'*; 'Cataplasm' was a legendary black cat believed in Elizabethan times to drink the blood of the injured or dying. He was accompanied by a bright red gnome called the Hemogoblin who would enter the homes of the sinful and rip their Band-Aids off very quickly.

[1197] *'Couch me awhile, and mark'*; the exact meaning of this odd phrase is uncertain. It is possible that in Shakespeare's time, 'couch' was a transitive verb, in which case Hamlet is suggesting that someone in the audience hit him repeatedly with a piece of living-room furniture, and then begin hitting someone named Mark.

Jess Borgeson as Hamlet;
A Piece of Foam Rubber as Yorick
While Jess often favorably compares his portrayal of Hamlet with those of Olivier, Gielgud, and McKellan, critics more often unfavorably compare him to his scene partner, shown here.

(GERTRUDE *and* LAERTES *enter, bearing the corpse of Ophelia—the dummy, wrapped in a sheet—and flowers.*)

D/LAERTES: Lay her in the earth; and from her fair
And unpolluted flesh, may violets spring.[1198]

A/GERTRUDE: Sweets to the sweet. Farewell.

D/LAERTES: Hold off the earth awhile,
'Til I have caught her once more in mine arms.

J/HAMLET *(leaping to the stage)*: What is he whose grief bears
such an emphasis?
This is I, Hamlet the Great Dane!

(*He spikes the skull of Yorick—it is rubber, and bounces away. He rushes to the corpse, and tries to yank it away from* LAERTES. *There is a brief tug of war over the corpse.*)

A/GERTRUDE: Gentlemen! Hamlet! Laertes!

D/LAERTES: The devil take thy soul.

(LAERTES *lets go of the corpse as* HAMLET *pulls, and it bonks* GERTRUDE *on the head.* GERTRUDE *exits, staggering.*)

[1198] *'may violets spring'*; at a period in history when everyone from beggar to monarch bathed with shocking infrequency, violets often grew on any skin exposed to full sunlight. The sentiment, then, is not as peculiar as it appears to us today.

The Compleat Wks of Willm Shkspr (Abridged)

J/HAMLET: I will fight with him until my eyelids no longer wag.
The cat will mew, the dog will have his day.[1199]
Give us the foils.

D/LAERTES: Come, one for me."

(GERTRUDE re-enters, hands a foil to each, then, as she exits:)

A/GERTRUDE: Now be careful. Those are sharp.

J/HAMLET: "Come, sir.

D/LAERTES: Come, my lord.

(They fence. HAMLET scores a hit.)

J/HAMLET: One.

D/LAERTES: No!

J/HAMLET: Judgment?

(ADAM enters. He is ostensibly CLAUDIUS, but is not quite totally dressed in three different costumes.)

A/CLAUDIUS: A hit, a hit; a very palpable hit."

DANIEL: What are you wearing?

ADAM: Hmmm. Let's play Guess What I Am Now. *(then, back in character:)*

[1199] *'the cat will mew, the dog will have his day'*; the association of Hamlet with the Great Dane makes the dog reference clear enough; why Laertes is identified as a cat less so. Rowe suggests that Laertes liked to sleep in impossibly contorted positions and stick his rear end in his master's face whenever possible.

A/CLAUDIUS: "Hamlet, here's to thy health. Drink off this cup.

J/HAMLET: Nay, set it by awhile," uncle... father... mother... whatever you are.[11180]

(They fence. HAMLET runs LAERTES completely through.)

"Another hit. What say you?

D/LAERTES *(examining the foil entering his chest and exiting his back)*: A touch. A touch, I do confess.

(GERTRUDE enters with a goblet.)

A/GERTRUDE: The queen carouses to thy fortune, Hamlet.[11181]

D/LAERTES: Madam, do not drink.

A/GERTRUDE: I will, my lord. I pray you pardon me.

D/LAERTES *(aside)*: It is the poisoned cup! It is too late.

(GERTRUDE chokes and exits.)

J/HAMLET: Come, for the third, Laertes."

[11180] *'whatever'*; the sexual ambiguity and role reversal cleverly used to comic effect by Adam throughout the show here comes to a head. The man who looks like a boy playing roles which in Shakespeare's time were played by boys disguised as women who in turn often had to dress like men is unquestionably Adam's actorly forté. 'It's historically accurate,' Long says. 'Besides, I kinda like wearing the dress.'

[11181] *'The queen carouses to thy fortune'*; an interesting twist on the already sexually-charged Oedipal relationship between the Prince and his mother is this indication that Hamlet may in fact have been pimping for the queen in his spare time, finding able-bodied young college chums to fulfill her boundless desire.

(They fence. HAMLET *drops his foil on the ground, and* LAERTES *continues fighting it.)*

J/HAMLET: Laertes, yo! Riposte, coupe, coup d'etat, cafe au lait, disarmez![11182]

(LAERTES' foil flies out of his hand and into HAMLET'S. LAERTES *picks up* HAMLET'S *foil, and they run each other through.)*

J/HAMLET AND D/LAERTES: Merde.

(Both fall. GERTRUDE *re-enters.)*

J/HAMLET: "How does the queen?[11183]

D/LAERTES: She swoons to see thee bleed.

A/GERTRUDE: No. The drink! The drink! I am poisoned. *(She dies dramatically, falls into* HAMLET'S *arms, who spins her offstage.)*

J/HAMLET: O villainy! Treachery! Seek it out!

D/LAERTES: It is here, Hamlet. Here I lie, never to rise again. I can no more. The king. The king's to blame.

(CLAUDIUS enters.)

[11182] *'cafe au lait, disarmez'*; Jess' knowledge of Latin is impressive; his French, less so.

[11183] *'How does the queen?'*; 'how does the queen *what?*' is the natural question. Oeufpate has proposed: 'How does the queen manage to co-govern the country, manage castle affairs and still have time for incest? She takes Geritol every day...'

J/HAMLET: What, the point envenom'd too? Then venom to thy
work!
Here, thou incestuous, murd'rous, cross-dressing Dane:
Follow my mother!

(HAMLET kills CLAUDIUS.)

D/LAERTES: Forgive me Hamlet. I am justly killed by mine own
treachery. *(Dies.)*

J/HAMLET: Heaven make thee free of it. *(He is dying too.)* I follow
thee.
(to the audience) You that look pale, and tremble at this chance
That are but mutes, or audience to this act;
If ever thou didst hold me in thy hearts
Absent thee from felicity awhile;
And in this harsh world draw thy breath in pain
To tell my story.[11184] The rest is silence. *(He gags, convulses,
then dies in a beautifully balletic pose.)*

*(Blackout. The lights come back up. JESS, ADAM AND DANIEL
bounce up and bow. They all exit, then return and bow again.
After a brief discussion:)*

ADAM: Very well, ladies and gentlemen. We will do it...

ALL: One more time!

[11184] *'tell my story'*; Hamlet, and the entire Royal Danish court at Elsinore, are
obviously a fairly sordid lot. By telling their story, the RSC in no way wishes to
imply that ALL Danes kill their brothers, marry their widows, usurp the throne,
drive their girlfriends to suicide, have their college buddies executed, poison their
wives, murder their nephews, and leave their country open to takeover by an
invading foreign power. However, just to be on the safe side, we encourage all
Danes to simply refrain from breeding so that their foul and hideous race may be
wiped from the face of the planet.

The Compleat Wks of Willm Shkspr (Abridged)

(JESS AND DANIEL reset the stage and clear props.)

ADAM: Ladies and gentlemen, that was 'The Complete Works of William Shakespeare,' but we have a few more minutes, so we're going to go through 'Hamlet' one more time, very quickly. I just want to make a brief announcement because we have some children in the audience. You've seen a lot of swords being used here, a lot of props flying back and forth, we make these things look simple, but really they're very difficult and very dangerous. Please, keep in mind that the three of us are trained professionals.

ALL: Do not try this at home!

ADAM: Yeah. Go over to a friend's house.

(Exeunt. A brief pause, then, at high speed, the actors re-enact the highlights of 'Hamlet,' matching the original staging and diction.)

J/HAMLET: "O that this too too solid flesh would melt.

D/HORATIO: My lord, I think I saw your father yesternight.

J/HAMLET: Would the night were come.

A/GHOST: Mark me!

J/HAMLET: Something is rotten in the state of Denmark.

A/GHOST: Revenge my murther.

D/LAERTES: My lord, this is strange.

J/HAMLET: Well, there are more things in heaven and earth so piss off. *(JESS slaps DANIEL.)*

J/HAMLET: To be or not to be, that is the—

A/OPHELIA: Good my lord!

J/HAMLET: Get thee to a nunnery!

A/OPHELIA: Aaaaugh!

J/HAMLET: Now, speak the speech trippingly on the tongue.

A/CLAUDIUS: Give o'er the play.[11185]

J/HAMLET: I'll take the ghost's word for a thousand pound. Now, mother, what's the matter?

A/GERTRUDE: Thou wilt not murder me. Help!

D/POLONIUS: Help! Help!

J/HAMLET: How now, a rat! Dead for a ducat, dead.

D/LAERTES: Now, Hamlet, where's Polonius?

J/HAMLET: At supper.

D/LAERTES: Where?

J/HAMLET: Dead.

[11185] *'Give o'er the play'*; literally, 'Give me the script—you're going so fast I can't keep up!'

The Compleat Wks of Willm Shkspr (Abridged)

A/OPHELIA *(splashing a cup of water in his face)*: Aaaaaaaaugh!

D/LAERTES: Sweet Ophelia!

J/HAMLET: Alas, poor Yorick! But soft, here comes the queen.

D/LAERTES: Lay her in the earth.

A/GERTRUDE: Sweets to the sweet.

D/LAERTES: Hold off the earth awhile.

J/HAMLET: It is I, Omelette the Danish.

D/LAERTES: The devil take thy soul.

J/HAMLET: Give us the foils.

D/LAERTES: One for me. O! I am slain!

A/GERTRUDE: O, I am poisoned.

J/HAMLET: I follow thee. The rest is silence.[11186]

(By now they all lay dead on the stage in the same death tableau as before. Pause. They all jump up for bows. They confer briefly.)

[11186] *'O that this too too solid flesh...The rest is silence'*; at the time of this publication, this section of the show holds the world record for the fastest performance of *Hamlet, the Tragedy of the Prince of Denmark*, at 42.2 seconds. The previous record was held by a Czechoslovakian company which performed the entirety of *Hamlet* between stops on a city bus in 48 seconds. In 1975, an East German company performed *Hamlet* in 18 seconds but the record was disallowed after their Ophelia tested positive for steroids.

JESS: Ladies and gentlemen, we shall do it FASTER!

(Exeunt. After a beat, HAMLET, LAERTES AND OPHELIA enter running, each with a deadly prop. All simultaneously scream a line, apply an instrument of death to themselves and fall dead. Pause, then all bounce up again for bows. ADAM exits, and JESS is halfway out the door.)

DANIEL: You've been fantastic, ladies and gentlemen. We shall do it BACKWARDS!

(JESS looks at DANIEL incredulously. ADAM re-enters. There is a brief heated discussion, then they all lie down—in the same death tableau .)

ADAM *(to the audience)*: You are very sick puppies!

JESS: Be sure to listen for the Satanic messages.

(Pause. Then the encore begins, and God be praised, it is an exact reversal of the lines, movement, gestures and blocking of the first encore, like a movie reel run backwards. Well, pretty nearly...)

J/HAMLET: Silence is rest the. Thee follow I.

A/GERTRUDE: Judas Priest is God!

D/LAERTES: Slain am I O!

J/HAMLET: Foils the us give. Dane the Hamlet, I is this.

D/LAERTES: Earth the off hold.

A/GERTRUDE: Sweets the to sweet.

The Compleat Wks of Willm Shkspr (Abridged)

D/LAERTES: Earth the in her lay.

J/HAMLET: Queen the comes here. Yorick poor, alas.

D/LAERTES: Ophelia sweet!

A/OPHELIA *(spitting a mouthful of water into a cup, and all over the audience)*: ghuaaaaaaA!

D/LAERTES: Father my is where?

J/HAMLET: Dead. Ducat a for dead.

D/POLONIUS: Help! Help!

A/GERTRUDE: Help! Me murder not wilt thou. Do thou wilt what.

J/HAMLET: Matter the what's, mother now?

DANIEL: Sesir gnik eht.

J/HAMLET: Tongue the on trippingly speech the speak.

A/OPHELIA *(spitting water out of his mouth, into a cup and all over the audience)*: Hguaaaaaa!

J/HAMLET: Nunnery a to thee get!

A/OPHELIA: Lord my good.

J/HAMLET: Be to not or be to.

(JESS slaps DANIEL backwards.)

Horatio, earth and heaven things in more are there.

D/HORATIO: Strange is this, lord my.

A/GHOST: Oob.

J/HAMLET: Denmark of state the in rotten is something.

D/HORATIO: Yesternight father your saw I think I, Lord my.

J/HAMLET: Melt would flesh solid too too this that O.

ALL: You thank![11187]

(All bow and exit.)

(All re-enter and bow.)

ADAM: Thank you, thank you, thank you, THANK YOU, THANK YOU!! THANK YOU!... *(audience quiets)* We just wanted to say thank you.

JESS: We wanted to let you know that we'll be performing... *(He plugs upcoming shows.)*

DANIEL: So if you enjoyed the show, tell your friends. If you didn't, tell your enemies.

ADAM: Thanks again for coming! I'm Adam—

[11187] *'Silence is rest the...You thank'*; the backwards version of *Hamlet* has been such a success that the RSC plans to apply the technique to other works. For example, the RSC's second full-length show, *The Complete History of America (abridged)*, begins with a picture of a nation in chaos, uncertain in direction, torn by internal strife, and questioning the viability of its own existence, and ends with the white man going back to Europe and minding his own damn business.

The Compleat Wks of Willm Shkspr (Abridged)

JESS: I'm Jess—

DANIEL: I'm Daniel, and we are—

ALL: The Reduced Shakespeare Company!

(All exit.)

(Lights come up. The audience is momentarily stunned. Then, slowly, they reach into their pockets, remove five- ten- and twenty-dollar bills, and throw them at the stage.)

The End[11188]

[11188]The End.

Appendices

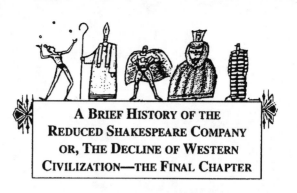

A Brief History of the Reduced Shakespeare Company or, The Decline of Western Civilization—the Final Chapter

Many scholars contend that the Reduced Shakespeare Company is the best thing that ever happened to an overrated dead playwright. True, we can safely say that the RSC's *The Complete Works of William Shakespeare (abridged)* is the greatest piece of drama in the history of the universe. And yet, social historians and cultural anthropologists worldwide are beginning to examine the possibility that behind the blinding brilliance of the RSC's fame and talent may lurk a dark and dreadful prophecy of doom.

Oswald Spengler, in his two-volume work, *The Decline of The West,* posits the theory that the fall of all great civilizations has been signalled by a tendency in the arts to adapt and rework past classical forms rather than create original work. The implications of this theory with regard to the Reduced Shakespeare Company are terrifying. Does the rise of the RSC star during the eighties and early nineties signal the twilight of Judeo-Christian Western civilization and herald the End of the World As We Know It? Or is the Reduced Shakespeare Company, as some have asserted, just a bunch of no-account doofuses? As the answers to these questions are of paramount importance to the fate of the human race, we would be well-advised to take a good hard look at the history of the Reduced Shakespeare Company.

The RSC was born in 1981, when Daniel Singer, a disgruntled drama student at the Guildford School near London, returned to his native California. Singer was busy learning the painful lesson that paid jobs performing classic plays in Northern California were scarce when he was inspired by a production of Tom Stoppard's *The (Fifteen-minute) Dogg's Troupe "Hamlet"* to write his own abbreviated version of Shakespeare's masterpiece. Singer held auditions for his four-person, half-hour *Hamlet* in August of that year. In his unassailable wisdom, he cast one Jess Borgeson, a disgruntled Shakespearean scholar at the University of California, Berkeley, in the lead role of Hamlet. Borgeson had just completed acting the role of the Melancholy Dane in a University production of Stoppard's reduction and claimed to be well-acquainted with Shakespearean abridgement techniques, such as deleting every other word of famous passages, e.g. Hamlet's "To be or not to be" soliloquy:

> "To or to that the.
> Whether is in mind
> suffer slings arrows outrageous;
> or take against sea troubles
> by end."

Borgeson seemed also to have deleted every other brain cell during his years in Berkeley, but he had a well-trimmed beard and his own tights, so Singer took the plunge.

No one was right for the role of Claudius, so Singer cast Michael Fleming, an energetic fellow who promised he would work hard, and whose Dumbo-like appearance while wearing the king's crown elicited howls of laughter even before he opened his mouth. (The tradition of ill-fitting headgear on flop-eared actors was to become an RSC trademark. See photo of Reed Martin, page 122.) Singer cast himself in the character roles of Horatio, Polonius and Laertes. The roles of Ophelia and Gertrude were filled by Barbara Reinertson, a blonde with a husky voice. Adam Long also auditioned that day, but as his boyish looks didn't seem appropriate for the Ghost and Claudius roles, he was ignored.

The day of the first performance at the Living History Centre's "Renaissance Pleasure Faire" in Novato, California, the actors voted on a name for the fledgling troupe. Among the choices were "Condensed (Just Add Water) Shakespeare Company," "Joseph Papp's New York Shakespeare Festival," and "The Reduced Shakespeare Company (RSC)." "Reduced Shakespeare Company"

The Original RSC - 1981
Daniel Singer, Michael Fleming, Barbara Reinertson
and Jess Borgeson

won by a landslide, and the first performance went off with a bang *and* a whimper.

This took place in 1981—the very same year in which Ronald Reagan and George Bush were sworn in as President and Vice-President of the United States of America. President Reagan is widely remembered for quadrupling the national debt, sleeping during Cabinet meetings and having a First Lady with a head the size of a medicine ball and an ego to match, but more to the point here, for heading an administration possessed of the unshakable belief that the end of civilization was nigh, that the United States and the Evil Empire of the Soviet Union would soon fight the battle of Armageddon, and that, to paraphrase then-Secretary of the Interior James Watt, we didn't need to practice environmental conservation because the Second Coming would be happening any day now and Christ Our Lord had no use for trees. (An inaccurate observation, incidentally. See the Gospel according to Irv, Chapter 10, verse 5, "and Jesus tied his ass to a tree and walked ten miles into Jerusalem." Ouch.)

Could the birth of the Reagan-Bush era and of the Reduced Shakespeare Company in *the same year* be mere coincidence? Or do they conspire to lead us toward the apocalyptic conclusion that the first signs of the end of all things were beginning to manifest their reality in the societal consciousness? When asked for his opinion on the subject, former President Reagan, contacted at the Reagan Presidential Library in Simi Valley, California, replied, "I don't recall, ask Mommy, Zzzzzzzzz....."

The four-person original RSC lasted exactly three weeks. In a parade at the Renaissance Faire, Miss Reinertson broke her ankle while dancing through a detailed recreation of an Elizabethan pothole. Singer called Borgeson during the week to report the bad news: "Barbara's broken her ankle. We'll have to cancel the shows."

"You know," Borgeson mused, "I've got a friend who's been watching every performance, is a quick study, and could probably learn Barbara's parts by this weekend."

"Great! What's her name?" Singer replied.

"Her name is Adam," Borgeson said. "We're gonna need a wig."

Adam Long was a childhood friend of Borgeson's from Thousand Oaks, California, where the two had attended Newbury Park High School together and formed an immediate bond in their common dislike of classmate Don Gellenbeck (his real name), who was a jock, a mental midget and a dickwad. The two youths collaborated on several theatrical works, including their acclaimed mythological epic in 20 minutes, "Sacs and Violins," and a 3-minute performance art piece, "Gellenbeck's Tiny Penis".

When Borgeson called asking him to join the RSC, Long was the disgruntled bass player in an acoustic punk rock band. Frustrated at trying to come up with an acoustic arrangement to the Sex Pistols' "Anarchy in the UK" and feeling that his talents were being wasted on an intellectually empty pursuit, Long jumped at the opportunity to put on a wig and a dress and fall down a lot while spouting Shakespearean verse.

The wig was procured and Long went onstage that weekend. Long's performance was, in a word, uncanny. One longtime fan recalls, "When he first came onstage, I thought, 'My God, what an ugly girl. He looks just like my mother.'" Long's performance was so terrifyingly authentic that Reinertson insisted on returning the following weekend, wearing a cast and hopping on one foot. The Company finished out the season with Long and Reinertson alternating shows, climaxing with a double-cast "Dueling Ophelias" extravaganza for the final performance. Barbara lost the duel. She had been replaced by an Ophelia with a Y chromosome.

With Long, the RSC quickly became famous for cross-dressing. Shall we consider this:

1) Indicative of the RSC's dedication to historical accuracy (women's roles were, after all, played by boys in Shakespeare's day); or

2) A decadent bourgeois Neroesque immoral Satanic Sodomite abomination prefacing the end of decency, righteousness,

and universal access to nacho cheese spread?

Many would argue the latter. Oblivius Maximus, an underrated Roman historian of the 3rd century C.E., in his famous oration "Posterios Graecorum Vincere" ("Kicking Greek Ass"), attributed the Roman eclipse of Classical Greek and Hellenic culture to the Greeks' effeminacy and low standards of sexual rectitude. In a stunning irony, Maximus was himself fascinated with "Posterios Graecorum," and was murdered in his bath by a jealous Greek slave boy named Tina.

In 1982, Borgeson returned to Berkeley to finish his English degree, leaving Long and Singer to carry the RSC banner. Adam penned a two-man version of *Romeo and Juliet*, and the two began performing anywhere and everywhere they possibly could: fairs, festivals, weddings, bar mitzvahs, car dealership blowouts, shopping mall openings, Young Republicans bake sales; no venue was left unsullied.

The next major turning point in the Company's history occurred when the Singer and Long were sharing a performance venue with the world-renowned juggling team *Sean and Robert*. These master manipulators made a seemingly lucrative living by passing the hat and soliciting donations after their performances. They taught the RSC the time-tested and unwritten (until now) equation of:

$$j/sec \times mph = \$ \to H$$

or, jokes per second times breakneck pace equals dollar bills in hat. More jokes, more bills. Better jokes, bigger bills. The RSC learned to apply the axioms of neuro-linguistic programming (e.g., "always mention God when asking for money") to *Romeo and Juliet*, transforming what had been a non-profit weekend hobby into an elaborate scheme to purloin spare change from feeble-minded yahoos.

Long and Singer called their former colleague and told him of the gambit, and of their average weekend haul. Borgeson's enthusiasm for the RSC quickly returned, and the three planned a revival of *Hamlet*. Several actors had come and gone in the roles of

The Two-Man RSC, 1983: Daniel and Adam

Ghost and Claudius; one morning the last in the series excused himself hurriedly when his daughter was born. The three-man Reduced Shakespeare Company was born the same day, and the troika worked *Hamlet* and *Romeo and Juliet* in repertory from 1985 to 1987.

In 1987, a friend suggested that the Company might find a welcome reception at the Edinburgh Festival Fringe in Scotland. Never having heard of the "Fringe," or the "Festival," or even of "Scotland" for that matter, the RSC researched the event and discovered that in order to perform in Edinburgh they would need a full-length show. Jack Tate, a fellow actor who admired the RSC, suggested that since they already knocked off two of the Bard's works in about 40 minutes, they could probably do *The Complete Works* in about an hour.

Tate is considered by many to be a genius. He was certainly considered so by the RSC, who showed no compunction in ripping off his idea post haste and booking a theater in Edinburgh under the description, "The Reduced Shakespeare Company presents *The Complete Works of William Shakespeare (abridged)*, all 37 plays by three actors in one hour." Pleased with themselves for their ingenuity and spunk, the three actors in question promptly celebrated, got drunk, woke up in the morning with purgatorial hangovers, realized they had to condense 35 five-act masterpieces of drama into 20 minutes, and became physically ill.

The Complete Works of William Shakespeare (abridged) received its first performance in a pre-Edinburgh tryout at the Paramount Ranch in Agoura, California on June 19, 1987. Exactly why the show premiered on the Old West set of a studio backlot is unclear now, but it seemed a good idea at the time. With the ghosts of John Wayne and Gary Cooper looking on in ethereal astonishment, the RSC blasted through the Bard's works to rapturous applause and standing ovations from all 350 corporeal beings there assembled. When asked whether he liked the show, the ghost of Cooper hauntingly mouthed the single syllable, "Nope." Wayne's ghost disappeared the instant Long put on a dress.

The Three-Man RSC, 1987: Adam, Jess and Daniel

By the time the Company arrived in Edinburgh two months later, its ranks had grown to five: Borgeson, Long and Singer, plus costume and prop goddess Sa Thomson and business manager Scott Ewing. Thomson was uniquely qualified for the demanding job: not only could she design and create stunning Elizabethan fashions and accessories on a shoestring budget and execute the lightning-fast changes backstage, but she often did so topless. Ewing had no such "great talents" to recommend himself, but nobody else seemed to want the job of business manager, so he came aboard. Ewing was and is an avid hunter.

The RSC's stint in Edinburgh was a fantastic success, earning rave reviews and widespread interest in the Company not only in the UK, but back home in California. Two performances of *The Complete Works* at Fringe Festival Los Angeles led to a six-week run at the Cast Theatre in Hollywood, where the show was expanded (some say "bloated") to a full two hours. The RSC then embarked on the first of many tours that have taken the Company to theaters all over the world, from the backwaters of New York, London, Dublin, Montreal, Tokyo and Melbourne to such cultural meccas as the Elkhart, Indiana Concert Club, the American Legion Hall in Templeton, California (the deathplace of L. Ron Hubbard, whose new book is due to be released any day now), and the Young Men and Women's Hebrew Association of North Jersey.

The RSC lineup metamorphosed in 1989 when founding member Singer retired to pursue a career as an "Imagineer" with the Walt Disney Company. The RSC hired UC Berkeley alumnus and disgruntled Ringling Bros./Barnum & Bailey clown Reed Martin to fill Singer's substantial codpiece. The Company spurted to new heights, climaxing in the March 1992 opening of an unlimited engagement at the Arts Theatre in London's West End.

Three months into the successful West End season, Borgeson, the last remaining member of the original Reduced Shakespeare Company, stunned his colleagues by quitting the troupe to run off with the often-topless prop and costume goddess Thomson. The troupe again turned to a UC Berkeley graduate to fill the vacancy,

The Compleat Wks of Willm Shkspr(Abridged)

The RSC, 1990, featuring Reed Martin's ears

hiring disgruntled frat boy-cum-director Austin Tichenor to play Borgeson's roles and to work on the Company's long-awaited second show—*The Complete History of America (abridged)*. Adam Long remains with the Company, wearing wigs and dresses and falling down a lot while spouting Shakespearean verse for the benefit of all sentient beings.

The meteoric rise into the theatrical stratosphere of the Reduced Shakespeare Company has undeniably prophetic overtones, but perhaps the question of whether their ascendance presages the fall of Western Civilization cannot be fully answered within the scope of this book. It is certainly disturbing that the RSC has attracted a substantial cult following, and that hundreds of thousands of ordinary God-fearing people have paid cash money to revel in the RSC's artistic excesses, but does this really mean the End of the World is nigh? Perhaps not, but consider this long-overlooked prediction of the 16th-century French seer and prophet Nostradamus:

> "When the Singer warbles a shorter tune
> And false locks and dresses are worn Long,
> Then he who mocks the Dane shall take up
>   with a seamstress,
> And Boom! The Earth shall be like unto toast."

The RSC today: Reed, Adam, and Austin Tichenor

A PAGE FROM WILLIAM SHAKESPEARE'S DIARY

by Jess Borgeson

While at the Eagle and Cherub Pub in Oxford last summer, where I was doing some very important academic research into the bottom of a pint of lager, I made an earth-shattering discovery. In a dark corner, stuck to the underside of a table with some bubble-gum, was a yellowed piece of parchment. I stretched up to remove it and found myself looking at what appeared to be two, but was actually one, authentic page from the diary of William Shakespeare. After much work deciphering the text, which was made difficult by the numerous scatological colloquialisms, I am able to present the first publication of this historic find.

MY DIARY
by Me, Will Shakspere
Greatest Playwright Ever

March 8, 1599

8:00 am. I am awakened by the malodorous breathing of Ben Jonson, a passable playwright but foul-mouthed, in speech and exhalation both. Verily, my hangover doth reverberate cannonlike in my pate. I wonder why fate hath dealt me such strange bedfellow?

8:01. Chris Marlowe burrows out from beneath the covers at the foot of the bed. Confused images from last night begin to congeal egglike in my pate. I remember a Dead Playwright's Society meeting, well-lubricated by piss-poor ale. I remember staggering back to my place for a game of strip nine-man's morris. I remember Marlowe, the loser, erotically licking Ben's bunionated big toe.

8:02. I feel ill.

8:03. One more forgotten participant of the night's debauch emergeth from the loo with a freshly-filled chamber pot. It be Good Queen Bess, who looked much sexier last night. Perhaps it was the wig.

8: 04. I vomit projectile-like in my pillow.

11:00. I rise and dress, deciding to take a miss on my traditional Spring bath this year. I do, howe'er, apply a liberal dose of my new hair tonic, a perky product called "Simply Slaphead."

11:15. I am late for rehearsal, so I decide to take the Tube. I am waiting impatiently at Hampstead station when a space alien landeth in a cigar-shaped vessel. He speaketh unto me, saying that I would have to wait three hundred years for the Northern Line to be built, and then another hundred for the arrival of a southbound Bank train. I decide to walk.

1:30 pm. I arrive two hours late at the Globe Theatre for a rehearsal of *A Midsummer Night's Dream*. Burbage, or as we affectionately call him, Dick, complaineth about the ass head he must wear as Bottom. "The prop-house could at least have cleaned out all the brains first—and the sinuses are still full of mulesnot!"

Burbage is rather a weenie, but what a lovely voice!

3:15. Rehearsal is interrupted by a travelling salesman peddling fire insurance. We send him packing, as the man who built the Globe assures us that thatched roof and live cannon are an excellent combination. We have a fascinating discussion about the use of irony in the opening lines of Henry V.

6:15. Supper with my dear old chum, Francis Drake. He is newly returned from the New World, and hath a brought me a souvenir: a flimsy garment with a strange motto thereon imprinted, which readeth, "MY FRIEND WENT TO THE NEW WORLD AND ALL I GOT WAS THIS STUPID T-SHIRT." I am mightily intrigued.

8:00. Royal Command Performance of *The Tragedy of Julius Caesar*. Sitting with the Queen in her box, I broach the subject of funding for my next production, *Hamlet*. Her Grace is unenthusiastic, and becometh positively penurious as *Caesar* progresses. She is particularly put out when the Roman Emperor, a reigning monarch, is stabbed on the Capitol steps. I play my trump card, threatening to blow the lid off the "Virgin Queen" hoo-hah if I don't get my funding. She draughteth a most savoury check, her mythical cherry intact.

11:45. I arrive home, weary from the day's exertions. As I crawl into bed, I sense that I am not alone. From 'tween the sheets, the throaty voice of Kit Marlowe whispereth, "Take all my love, my love, yea take it all."

11:45:30. I take all of Marlowe's love.

11:46. I knit up the ravell'd sleave of care.

The RSC and Critical Consensus:
"Comic Genius" or "Whoopee Cushions with Legs?"

Since William Shakespeare's death in 1616, his life and work have been the subject of more critical debate and dissent than any other subject in the history of the arts—with the possible exception of the provocative question, "Just how short *was* Henri Toulouse-Lautrec?" The line of inquiry begins with the primordial question, "Did Shakespeare really exist, or were his plays written by a monkey at a typewriter?" It continues unabated through "How old is Hamlet?" and "What the hell is Gertrude doing in her closet?" and ends...with the Reduced Shakespeare Company.

The very first critical notice of the Reduced Shakespeare Company appeared in the *San Francisco Examiner* during the troupe's infancy in 1981. Reviewer Nancy Scott, spending a day at the Renaissance Pleasure Faire, had this to say about the fledgling RSC:

> They are to your ordinary product as
> prosciutto is to ham in the can. It's clever.
> It's remarkably silly. It's a great send-up of
> Shakespeare.

It was to be six years before another major newspaper wrote about the Reduced Shakespeare Company, but this early notice gives a distilled view of the debate that was to rage in the world press about the troupe and *The Complete Works of William Shakespeare* ever after. Is it clever? Is it just plain silly? Or is it really, at a deeper level, a metaphor for food? (See footnotes to *Hamlet*.) The critics have been polarized on these questions. With one notable exception, which we will be singling out for ridicule and revulsion later on, the RSC has had little cause to complain about its treatment by the critics. Most have at least deemed the performers personally "likeable," even if they found the show "appalling." But the polarity of the debate, and the fierceness with which some reviewers have staked out their ground, is illuminating.

First, a word about the subjectivity of theatrical criticism. In this post-Einsteinian world, we know that all experience is, at some level, relative; especially those experiences of existence related to our perception of art, beauty, truth, and of course, time. To illustrate: the first encore to *Hamlet* in the *Complete Works* has remained essentially unchanged since its debut in 1981. It has always clocked in at about 45 seconds, give or take a second or two depending on how much coffee Adam has consumed before the show. And yet, here is how the following publications have clocked it:

San Francisco Examiner	4 minutes
Time Out (London)	3 minutes
Canadian Press	2 minutes
News-Herald (Bloomington, Indiana)	90 seconds
Honolulu Advertiser	45 seconds
Festival Times (Scotland)	39 seconds
Entertainment Today (U.S.)	12 seconds
Sunday Press (Melbourne, Australia):	5 seconds

Only the *Honolulu Advertiser* got the time right: "Othello in the space of 45 seconds!" they marvelled. How they came to the conclusion that the guy saying "to be or not to be" and talking to a skull was Othello, the Moor of Venice, is another question entirely.

The Compleat Wks of Willm Shkspr(Abridged)

Yet this temporal distortion only scratches the surface of the controversy surrounding the show. For example, would Shakespeare approve of the RSC's interpretation of his work? "Shakespeare must be spinning in his grave" is the lead of Sylvie Drake's scathing 1989 review in the *Los Angeles Times*. But the glowing assessment of the same performance in *Variety* confidently asserts, "There is no doubt that W.S., himself a great lover of the wink and nod, would approve."

Why the disagreement? Where are the battle lines drawn? Is anyone still reading this article?

Some argue that the differences are largely geographical. The RSC had great success in its early days on the West Coast. In addition to the *San Francisco Examiner*, The *Los Angeles Times* was an avid supporter. "Complete Shakespeare Complete Fun," trumpeted the RSC's first headline review by Robert Koehler, who beamed that the show would "tickle anyone who's ever squirmed through dry classroom Shakespeare." The Orange County edition of the *Times* later called the Company "whoopee cushions with legs" and "one giant stupid human trick," which the RSC took as a compliment. So far, the Company was flying high, with nary a bad review to its name. The Los Angeles *Daily News* even inoculated the Company against any future bad reviews by declaring *The Complete Works* "Fast-paced, continually clever, an exhilarating mix of highbrow and lowbrow that will appeal to all but the stuffiest adults."

The RSC was about to encounter that "stuffiest of adults" in the form of *Los Angees Times* reviewer Sylvie Drake (affectionately known in the Los Angeles theatrical community as "that @#$%! bitch"). The RSC had been planning to take up permanent residence in its hometown of Los Angeles, open a big splashy high-publicity run in Beverly Hills, get a load of commercial offers, film roles, maybe a Nike endorsement, definitely a talk show; Sylvie Drake had other ideas for the local yokels. "A SHAKESPEAREAN COMEDY OF ERRORS" was the headline over which Sylvie (now affectionately known to the RSC as "that @#$%! bitch") vented her considerable spleen. "Overextended slapstick with as much padding as it takes to stuff a Falstaff...Much ado about nothing," she wrote, along with suggestions that the performers grow up and get real jobs. Such is the power of the *Los Angeles Times* that, despite the earlier glowing reviews from the same paper, the RSC was banished, Cordelia-like, from the L.A. scene. The troupe tied a handkerchief filled with props and costumes to a stick, slung it over its collective shoulder (where it neatly lodged in a large chip) and left their beloved home for tours of Australia, Canada, Ireland and New Jersey. "Let's hope comedy this raw is as they like it those regions," Drake added as a bon voyage.

New Jersey, the first stop on the RSC's Banishment Tour, was skeptical. The *Princeton Packet* logged the first East Coast review of the show:

> What passes for inspired zaniness on the
> West Coast may strike more sophisticated
> East Coast audiences as just plain silly...
> Sometimes less is more. But not this time.

That New Jersey elitist was apparently much "more sophisticated" than Mel Gussow of *The New York Times*, who took the opposite tack: "This troupe does more with less...The pithier-than-Python parodies defolio Shakespeare...Irresistible."

The further the RSC travelled from Los Angeles, the more well-received they tended to be. The *Montreal Gazette* pronounced *The Complete Works of William Shakespeare (abridged)* "The funniest show you are likely to see in your entire lifetime." In Melbourne, Australia, the RSC learned the value of granting sexual favors to critics when reviewer Fiona Scott-Norman called the show "The most physical, imaginative and hysterical rendition of any of the Bard's works you are likely to see." She also insightfully noted that the show contained "Lots of physical bendy stuff." The Honolulu Star-Bulletin opined, "This crew would be funny interpreting a telephone book." So far, Sylvie's farewell curse was the troupe's blessing.

Then, in 1990, the RSC applied the supreme test of geography to critical opinion by tackling the Bard on his home turf: London. Filled with trepidation as to how a nation presumably filled with Shakespeare 'purists' of the Sylvie Drake variety would respond to the loose-lipped antics of these American "cultural guerrillas," the Company looked with fear at their first reviews.

"Who says Americans can't do Shakespeare?", trumpeted *The Guardian*, indicating an enthusiastic welcome for the RSC in England that was to surpass their wildest imaginings. *Time Out* noted:

> Shakespeare scholars should be compelled
> to watch this. For pace, dexterity and wit
> I've seldom seen better. A high-powered,
> Will-powered evening forsooth.

The *Daily Telegraph* made the RSC Critic's Choice; *The Independent* even went this far:

> On the principle that that imitation is the
> sincerest form of flattery, this paper should
> perhaps offer a specially speeded up review:
> "Absl hlrs (Ind.)"

The reviews from the Shakespurists of that sceptered isle, that England, were fairly unanimous in their approbation of the RSC. England had been conquered, and Sylvie Drake could go suck a fountain pen.

And yet, even in agreement, the reviews differ shockingly on major issues of the Reduced approach. For example, at what intellectual level does the material in the show operate? Many a critic has labelled the script "sophomoric." "Collegiate" is the assessment of the *Los Angeles Times* and *New York Daily News*. *Newsday* at least bestows a diploma when it describes the company as "big sloppy puppies with bachelor degrees." At the extremes, *Variety* plumbs the depths by likening the show to "a smart-alecky teen who doesn't know when it's time to shut up, already," while a Dublin paper launches the troupe into the intellectual stratosphere with "positively PhD!" Personally, the Company favors the assessment of the *Montreal Gazette*, which cautiously posits that the show is "Much more intelligent than it appears to be at first..."

Critics have also offered widely disparate guesses as to the Company's comic influences: The *L.A. Weekly* calls the troupe "Part Three Stooges, part Smothers and Marx Brothers and part circus clowns." *The Guardian* accuses the RSC of being under the influence of "Monty Python, the Marx Brothers, Mel Brooks and cannabis." "Bugs Bunny," says one paper; "Buster Keaton, Harpo Marx and The Three Stooges," suggests another. The Marx Brothers seem to keep popping up, sometimes in unusual fashion: "A Marxist interpretation of [Shakespeare's] Comedies is perfectly valid, even if it is Harpo, Groucho and Chico rather than Karl," theorizes *The Scotsman*. Perhaps the most unusual comparison in trying to describe the RSC's comic style comes from the *Honolulu Star-Bulletin*: "Picture Mikhail Gorbachev in a tutu..."

Most reviewers agree that the RSC is "parodying," "pulverizing," "lampooning," "bastardizing," "skewering," "scissoring" or "deconstructing" the Bard's work, and Drake's assertion, that Shakespeare's quiet rest in his Stratford grave is endangered by the Company's work, is commonplace. Yet many others believe exactly the opposite, like London's *What's On*:

> The RSC may mock Shakespeare but at the same time acknowledge his genius. The show they produce is not dissimilar to Shakespeare in his own time—men in women's clothing, loud audience participation—long before the hushed respectful silence of the great tomb of the Barbican.

And what about the Barbican, and its tenants: the "other"

RSC, the Royal Shakespeare Company? How do the critics draw the obvious comparison? Again, opinions are disparate. On the occasion of the London opening of *The Complete Works*, The *Evening Standard* wished the Reduced a short run, doubting that London would "find room for two RSC's," while *City Limits* found the American RSC "so entertaining that you wonder whether you'll ever enjoy their Stratford namesakes' productions again."

But perhaps the most telling evidence of the dissent among the critics regarding the Reduced Shakespeare Company is the fact that they have stopped merely praising or bashing the RSC, and have begun, sickeningly, to turn on each other. Gerard van Werson, writing in London's *The Stage*, takes the RSC and his critical colleagues equally to task:

> [Are these] witless amateurs...the same
> fellows who received sell-out notices at the
> Edinburgh Fringe? Against all this, bad
> acting and bad reviewing, may angels and
> ministers of grace defend us.

The debate, having now turned inward on itself, will rage on. At its current rate of proliferation, in fact, the pages of criticism devoted to the Reduced Shakespeare Company will soon outstrip those devoted to Shakespeare himself. We must wonder, is there really any consensus to be found here, or is the debate quite literally academic? If we "witless amateurs" of the RSC are to come down on any particular side of the greatest controversy in the history of the arts, our opinion would have to be this:

Henri Toulouse-Lautrec was very, very short indeed.

About The Authors

Jess Borgeson

Jess retired from the RSC in July, 1992. He now lives with his wife Sa in Los Angeles, writing for film and television and editing bogus academic texts under the fraudulent pseudonym "Professor J. M. Winfield." He spends most of his spare time in a single-minded quest to mix the perfect martini.

Adam Long

Born in Manhattan, and raised in Southern California with Texans, Adam now resides in London with his lovely wife, Alex, and a small grey rabbit named Willard. He cites his influences as Harpo Marx, Dogen Zenji, and the Grateful Dead.

Daniel Singer

Originally from Santa Rosa, California, Daniel wasted his twenties on a silly acting troupe until finally achieving his dream career as a theme-park designer at Walt Disney Imagineering. Visitors to Disneyland may see a correlation between his work on "Toontown" and his contributions to the RSC. Daniel lives in Los Angeles with a handsome bearded gentleman. They are "confirmed bachelors."

MAESTRO, PLEASE!

Cartoons by Ed Fisher

Here is a cartoon album sure to bring a smile and a bravissimo from classical music buffs and concertgoers everywhere. From the pages of *The New Yorker, Punch, Harpers, Opera Quarterly* and others, Ed Fisher fans will embrace anew his mad and passionate composers, his slightly lunatic contraltos and all other delightful characters of his eitty world of Serious Music.

paper • ISBN 1–55783–108–4

SHAKESCENES: SHAKESPEARE FOR TWO

The Shakespeare Scenebook

EDITED AND WITH AN INTRODUCTION
BY JOHN RUSSELL BROWN

Thirty-five scenes are presented in newly edited texts, with notes which clarify meanings, topical references, puns, ambiguities, etc. Each scene has been chosen for its independent life requiring only the simplest of stage properties and the barest of spaces. A brief description of characters and situation prefaces each scene and is followed by a commentary which discusses its major acting challenges and opportunities.

paper ▌ ISBN 1-55783-049-5

SHAKESPEARE'S PLAYS IN PERFORMANCE
by John Russell Brown

In this volume, John Russell Brown snatches Shakespeare from the clutches of dusty academics and thrusts him centerstage where he belongs—in performance.

Brown's thorough analysis of the theatrical experience of Shakespeare forcibly demonstrates how the text is brought to life: awakened, colored, emphasized, and extended by actors and audiences, designers and directors.

"A knowledge of what precisely can and should happen when a play is performed is, for me, the essential first step towards an understanding of Shakespeare."
—*from the Introduction by John Russell Brown*

paper•ISBN 1-55783-136-X•

THE BRUTE

AND OTHER FARCES
By Anton Chekhov
Edited by Eric Bentley

"INDISPENSABLE!"
— Robert Brustein
Director, Loeb Drama Center
Harvard University

The blustering, stuttering eloquence of Chekhov's unlikely heroes has endured to shape the voice of contemporary theater. This volume presents seven minor masterpieces:

THE HARMFULNESS OF TOBACCO
SWAN SONG
A MARRIAGE PROPOSAL
THE CELEBRATION
A WEDDING
SUMMER IN THE COUNTRY
THE BRUTE

paper • ISBN: 1-55783-004-5

SOLILOQUY!

The Shakespeare Monologues
Edited by Michael Earley and Philippa Keil

At last, over 175 of Shakespeare's finest and most performable monologues taken from all 37 plays are here in two easy-to-use volumes (MEN and WOMEN). Selections travel the entire spectrum of the great dramatist's vision, from comedies and romances to tragedies, pathos and histories.

"Soliloquy is an excellent and comprehensive collection of Shakespeare's speeches. Not only are the monologues wide-ranging and varied, but they are superbly annotated. Each volume is prefaced by an informative and reassuring introduction, which explains the signals and signposts by which Shakespeare helps an actor on his journey through the text. It includes a very good explanation of blank verse, with excellent examples of irregularities which are specifically related to character and acting intentions. These two books are a must for any actor in search of a 'classical' audition piece."

ELIZABETH SMITH
Head of Voice & Speech
The Juilliard School

paper•MEN: ISBN 0-936839-78-3 • WOMEN: ISBN 0936839-79-1

THE ACTOR'S MOLIÈRE

A New Series of Translations for the Stage by

Albert Bermel

THE MISER and GEORGE DANDIN

ISBN: 0-936839-75-9

❋

THE DOCTOR IN SPITE OF HIMSELF and THE BOURGEOIS GENTLEMAN

ISBN: 0-936839-77-5

❋

SCAPIN and DON JUAN

ISBN: 0-936839-80-5